RED THREAD

*A Spiritual Journal of Accompaniment,
Trauma and Healing*

by Jennifer Atlee-Loudon

EPICA

Copyright © 2001 by EPICA
The Ecumenical Program on Central America and the Caribbean
1470 Irving Street NW
Washington, DC 20010
(202) 332-0292; fax (202) 332-1184
e-mail: epica@igc.org
web page: www.epica.org

An EPICA Book

Library of Congress Cataloging-in-Publication Data

Atlee-Loudon, Jennifer, 1962-
  Red thread: a spiritual journal of accompaniment, trauma and healing / by
  Jennifer Atlee-Loudon. p. cm.
  Includes bibliographical references.
  ISBN 0-918346-25-8 (pbk.)
    1. Atlee-Loudon, Jennifer, 1962---Diaries. 2. Christian biograpghy--
Nicaragua. 3. Christian biograpghy--United States. 4. Nicaragua--Politics and
government--1990- I. Title.

BR1725.A84 A3 2001
277.285'0828'092--dc21
[B]   00-052780

Front cover: *Re-member us you who are living, restore us, renew us. Speak for
our silence. Continue our work. Weave the web of peace.* "Re-member Us,"
etching by Judith Anderson, photo by Jim Colando
Back cover: photo by Terry Foss
Book Design by Ann Butwell/EPICA
Editing by Marilu MacCarthy/EPICA
Proofreading by Siobhán Dugan

DEDICATION

This book is dedicated to the people
whose stories are told in its pages, and
to Tom – for sharing this journey and
for his constant love and encouragement.

ACKNOWLEDGEMENTS

My deepest thanks to:
Carmen and Olivia for their gifts of life,
Ron and Betsy for their constant support,
Rita for being a mother to so many,
Jeanette for helping me to understand the process of
trauma and recovery from political violence, and
the many healers who have shared their gifts
and wisdom, especially Clara
who cares for my soul.

Finally, thanks to
Marilu for her careful and diligent work as editor
and to all at EPICA.

MAP OF NICARAGUA

CONTENTS

FOREWORD

I am delighted to be able to introduce Jennifer Atlee-Loudon's, *Red Thread: A Spiritual Journey of Accompaniment, Trauma and Healing.* I well remember meeting Jennifer, a pleasant round-faced woman working in the acupuncture clinic in Achuapa, Nicaragua with the extraordinary peasant healer, Flor de Maria. I still have the photos I took on that occasion. I was there with a study group of students. We were being escorted by my friend, Mayra Sirias, a plucky young woman who had been a Sandinista militant since the age of fourteen. I had been in Nicaragua earlier, in the days of the Revolution, and we were depressed to see how quickly the fragile gains in education, cooperatives and health care were being dismantled by the new government that the United States had helped to install with enormous bribery money and threats of continued war and embargo.

Mayra was showing us how some of the women's work was surviving through independent centers, no longer aided by the government. In the women's center in Achuapa, where we had spent two days, there were classes in reproductive health, leadership training and literacy. We were brought to Flor's clinic as an example of a local "miracle," how a peasant woman, herself healed by acupuncture from a visiting Japanese monk, had become the main healer in a town where the health clinics created by the revolution had been defunded. Flor's healing capacities seemed truly magical. With her combination of herbal medicine and acupuncture, she seemed to be able to transform impossible cases of paralysis and broken bones into healthy bodies with smiling faces.

Like Jennifer, I share a deep unquenchable anger at the historical crime committed by the United States against the Nicaraguan people. This crime goes back to our abusive treatment of this tiny country in the nineteenth century, continued in our occupation of the country for 20 years and then the installation and support of the brutal Somoza dictatorship for another 43 years. This infamous history was climaxed by our country's determination to destroy the fragile Sandinista revolution that swept the country in 1979 after so many years of

oppression propped up by the United States. The first years of the revolution were exhilarating -- the literacy campaign that taught people throughout the country to read and installed popular education centers, the parallel health campaign that set in place people's health clinics, the distribution of land to cooperatives.

But soon the brutal reality of the contra war set in, funded overtly and covertly by the intolerably bigoted and stupid Reagan regime, incapable of seeing the Nicaraguans as people worthy of directing their own lives, only able to see this valiant effort through the demonizing lens of "communist infiltration." I was in Nicaragua on the eve of the 1990 election. We could see everywhere the evidence of American funding of the cobbled-together "UNO" coalition headed by Violeta Chamorro. Fancy trucks and equipment bought with this money, funds to buy votes, were abundant. Behind these funds lay the terrible threat of continued war and embargo. The shelves in the stores were empty, parts to repair trucks and machinery lacking, thanks to the tight grip imposed on outside imports. Still the spirit of the Sandinistas was high, and our group, too, assumed they would win.

I too was shocked to learn in February 1990 that they had lost the election, although the Sandinistas still held the majority in the parliament, whose democratic constitution they had put in place. It was evident that the people, especially the women, were war weary: tired of sons, brothers and husbands being killed, tired of the embargo, tired of the endless spin of death and destruction. By that time, unfortunately, the corruption of key Sandinista leaders was already showing, their determination to hang on to some power and benefits, the famous "canastas" of wealth they carried out of office with them, their willingness to sell out the people to maintain a foothold in government.

Already when we visited in 1992, the evidence of the new capitalist regime was evident. In downtown Managua, a new shopping center had sprung up, filled with the toys of a consumer society, available only to the rich. Privatization of health and education were setting in. The returned Somocistas from Miami were determined to take back their lands from the peasant cooperatives. The IMF was making its annual visit to impose impossible policies on the Nicaraguan government in order to pay back the unpayable debt through dismantling investment in the welfare of the people.

This history of Nicaragua's treatment by the United States was symbolized for me by the judgment of the World Court. In the last days of the Sandinista regime, Miguel d'Escoto, Maryknoll priest and Secretary of State, had the brilliant idea of taking a grievance procedure to the World Court at the Hague, charging the United States with crimes of unprovoked intervention and destruction of Nicaragua. The World Court ruled in Nicaragua's favor, declaring the minimum damages that the United States should pay to Nicaragua at $17 billion. This decision was scarcely reported in the U.S. press. The United States government treated it with contempt, as we do with all international decisions that go against what we define as "our interests."

But the decision stung, and the U.S. government was determined to erase it. One of the conditions for supporting the new Chamorro regime was that the President repudiate all claim to this money, with promises of U.S. aid instead. This promise was soon ignored. The story of the decision of the World Court is one that must not be forgotten. It must be told again and again, to help make U.S. Americans understand that not just a few "crazies" took the Sandinista side, but the overwhelming opinion of the world, represented by the World Court.

The question remains: why was the United States so determined to destroy these fragile but hopeful efforts of Nicaraguans to better their lives? Camilo Dufresno, a priest who served as administrator for the Maryknoll Sisters in Managua, summed up for me the reason: "they had to destroy the threat of a good example." In other words, what was threatening about the Nicaraguan revolution was not that it detracted materially from American investments in Nicaragua, which were few, or that "communists" were about to land on the Texas borders, but that it might provide a ray of hope to other impoverished peoples in Latin America and elsewhere that an alternative, democratic socialist way of "development" is possible.

This possibility stood against our national religion; namely, that only the neo-liberal capitalist economy and world market "works." All other alternatives are impossible, contrary to the "natural law" and the will of God, and are doomed to lead to poverty and tyranny. We make this ideology a basic tenet of our foreign policy. By intervention, low intensity warfare and embargo we aim to impoverish and destroy any country seeking an alternative in order to "prove" our prediction of their inevitable fate. This is the key to our brutal destruction of the Sandinista revolution in the 1990's. Sad to say, we did the job of destroying the threat of a good example so well, with collaboration from the Nicaraguan elites, that today its brief accomplishments can scarcely be remembered. Nicaragua is now one of the poorest countries in Central America and the Caribbean, exceeded only by Haiti. Hope itself has been all but extinguished.

This is why it is so important to remember the revolution, to refuse to let its history be erased, along with the whitewashing of the murals that heralded its vision. The memory of its hopes, brief accomplishments, struggle and vision must be kept alive. For it is from the root of memory that new sprouts can some day come forth. This is the importance of the publication of Jennifer's journal of her experiences in the years of the revolution and its aftermath. It keeps the memory alive. It keeps the fragile flame of hope burning in the midst of the apparent triumph of the powers of evil. This is resurrection hope, from which new life is again and again reborn.

—Rosemary Radford Ruether

HISTORICAL BACKGROUND

The history of U.S. involvement in Nicaragua is a long and complex one. As far back as the 19th century, interventions began in the name of "U.S. interests," mostly for commercial purposes. This includes the outrageous actions of the notorious mercenary, William Walker. In 1855, he hired an army, invaded Nicaragua and declared himself president. He was recognized by the government in Washington in order to secure the rights to a canal for the United States. Two years later, Walker was overthrown and constitutional rule reestablished.

Starting in 1912, the U.S. Marines occupied Nicaragua for more than 20 years until 1933, during which time the United States claimed Nicaragua as a protectorate. In 1927, the Marines struggled to put down an uprising led by Augusto Cesar Sandino who had organized a popular army of workers and peasants to try to overthrow the rule of the Nicaraguan oligarchy. This uprising was principally nationalistic and anti-imperialist in character.

U.S. President Franklin D. Roosevelt was thwarted in winning this war outright. He subsequently focused on training the Nicaraguan National Guard, maintaining control over it, and, in 1936, putting the first of two infamous Anastasio Somozas into power as president, leading to a 43-year family dictatorship. It was the first Anastasio Somoza who arranged the assassination of Sandino in 1934. During this period, the United States benefited from access to Nicaragua's natural resources and cheap labor. Throughout the Marine occupation and the Somoza family dictatorship however, the Nicaraguan people continued resisting, organizing and pressing for social change. The Somoza dictatorships were notoriously brutal in their efforts to eliminate popular resistance yet the people persisted in their quest. In July 1979 after an eighteen-year struggle, the armed opposition named after their hero of the 1920s, the Sandinista Front for National Liberation (FSLN or Frente), celebrated the overthrow of the second Dictator Anastasio Somoza, and installed a revolutionary government.

Despite a lack of experience in government, inheriting a war-torn, bankrupt, indebted country and a legacy of underdevelopment, in three years the Sandinista Revolution made remarkable, measurable advances:

♦ More than 40,000 landless rural farmers received access to land on which to grow food for the first time.
♦ Production of basic food crops increased.
♦ Export crop production increased.
♦ Consumption of basic food soared.
♦ Food self-sufficiency was at hand.
♦ Infant mortality rate was cut by one third.
♦ Incidence of malaria was reduced by one third.
♦ Vaccination campaigns protected over one million Nicaraguans against preventable diseases.
♦ Illiteracy was dramatically reduced and 40% of the population was involved in formal schooling.[1]

The success of the Sandinista Revolution empowered other revolutionary movements that were fighting against the status quo in Central America, particularly the armed struggles in El Salvador and Guatemala. By 1981, the United States government under President Reagan was irretrievably

---

[1] Collins, Joseph with Frances Moore Lappe and Nick Allen. *What Difference Could a Revolution Make: Food and Farming in the New Nicaragua.* Institute for Food and Development Policy, 1982, p.4

committed to fighting all these populace-based guerilla movements in each of the countries. Reagan framed the justification as an East-West confrontation with the demonized Soviet Union and its puppet Cuba posing the "threat of world Communism at the backdoor of the United States."

In Nicaragua, President Reagan began supporting Somoza's ex-National Guard – the *contras* – with arms and training in an attempt to overthrow the revolution. They based themselves in Honduras and Costa Rica and from there carried out raids against the Nicaraguan people. As the war escalated, the energy of the Sandinista government was increasingly directed into defense. By the late 1980s, many of the leaders and promoters of social programs had been killed and the achievements of the Revolution were being eroded. In 1990, after ten years of war, national elections resulted in a victory for the opposition candidate, Violeta Chamorro, and the end of the *contra* war.

In the 1990s at the conclusion of the armed struggles in Guatemala and El Salvador, truth commissions were established as part of the peace process to help society come to terms with the violence that occurred in the previous decades. People have argued that the whole truth must be told – that of the victims and also that of the perpetrators – because a new future cannot be built if the past is not fully acknowledged and responsibility for abuse assumed. No such truth commission has yet been established in Nicaragua.

INTRODUCTION

In 1985, I spent a few weeks in Washington, D.C. helping Witness for Peace[2] participate in a congressional hearing on U.S. policy and the *contra* war to overthrow the Sandinista Revolution in Nicaragua. While I was there a group of U.S. war veterans, three from Vietnam and one World War II vet, called an urgent prayer meeting. I remember sitting in a circle listening intently as those men shared what they were feeling as the war intensified in Nicaragua. Some of them said they were seeing Vietnam again, feeling Vietnam in their bodies, living Vietnam again. They were remembering – and their memories compelled them to act.

Within weeks, those vets had declared a Fast for Life on the steps of the nation's Capitol. They went to the Vietnam War Memorial and returned their Medals of Honor – they left them on the wall – and said "There is no honor in this – this is a disgrace – we are ashamed of this." Barely ten years after the U.S. pullout from Vietnam, the veterans were responding to the military strategy called "low intensity warfare," perfected in Vietnam and now being employed in Nicaragua, and they were making an appeal to the people of the United States to "own" their collective responsibility for the government's abuses of power.

---

[2] Witness for Peace (WFP)- an organization formed in 1983 to maintain a permanent presence of U.S. people in the war zones of Nicaragua to witness the violence carried out on the civilian population by the contras, the U.S. funded counter-insurgency army made up of Dictator Somoza's ex-National Guardsmen.

Dr. Derek Summerfield of the Medical Foundation for the Care of Torture Victims explains the military strategy known as "low intensity warfare" in this way,

Population is the target – through systematic violence and terror, the aim is to penetrate into homes, families and the entire social fabric of grassroots social relations. It is a science of warfare whose goal is controlling the qualitative aspects of human life to produce demoralization and paralysis. Terror is sown not just randomly but also through targeted assaults on health workers, teachers, cooperative leaders, anyone whose work symbolizes shared values and aspirations. Torture, mutilation and execution in front of family members are routine.[3]

Low intensity warfare entails high intensity suffering on the part of civilian populations. As a result of the changing nature of warfare, 90% of the casualties in recent armed conflicts have been civilians. (In World War I, 5% of the total casualties were civilians, 50% in World War II, and over 80% in Vietnam.)[4] However, there is a "low" political risk for the perpetrators who can distance themselves from responsibility for political violence through the use of proxy forces, as in the case of the *contras.* This abnegation of responsibility by the authors makes the role of witnesses to political violence an important one.

In her classic work, *Trauma and Recovery,* Judith Herman states that those who have been witness to political violence are caught in the conflict between perpetrator and victim.

---

[3] Summerfield, Dr. Derek. *"The Psychosocial Effects of Conflict in the Third World: A Short Study."* November 1990. OXFAM AMERICA. Boston, p. 1.
[4] Ibid. Dr. Summerfield's article cites the International Symposium of Children and War, 1983.

It is morally impossible to remain neutral in this conflict... It is very tempting to take the side of the perpetrator. All that the perpetrator asks is that the bystander do nothing – appealing to the universal desire to hear and speak no evil. The victim, on the contrary, asks the bystander to share the burden of pain. The victim demands action, engagement, remembering.[5]

A war is not over when the weapons are laid down. The psychosocial wounds require healing. Part of that healing is a telling of what happened – who did what to whom – so that the patterns of abuse are revealed and not repeated. This truth telling is the basis from which responsibility for abuses can be assumed so that reconciliation and true peace can be built.

Being a witness also requires one to heal the burden of pain that one absorbs from exposure to violent events. The healing process leads one from brokenness to wholeness, victimization to re-empowerment, from paralysis to advocacy. I have experienced the unfolding of this process in myself and in many Nicaraguan friends. However, I have also seen many whose psycho-spiritual wounds from traumatic events remain unprocessed – impacting their present and their future.

Summerfield states that the recounting of traumatic events is fundamental to the process of personal healing and recovery.[6] This journal is the telling of the political violence that I saw. It is in no way the whole story – many other stories need to be told. Rather it is one person's experience of the impact of U.S. policy of "low intensity warfare" on the people of Nicaragua with whom I lived and worked. As a U.S. citizen whose government sponsored this violence, it is my responsibility to the victims to tell the truth that I lived.

---

[5]Herman, Judith, M.D. *Trauma and Recovery: The Aftermath of Violence, from Domestic Abuse to Political Terror.* Basic Books, 1997, p. 7.

[6] Summerfield, Dr. Derek. op. cite. p. 14.

This journal is the telling of the healing process that unfolded in my life. A glimpse of the paschal mystery has been revealed to me in the fact that it was the "victims" themselves – friends I lost – who insisted that I remember, engage, and act. They visited me in dreams, surrounded me with their presence, urging me to get up, go on, find hope, tell their story and work for a true peace in myself and in the world. Dreams have been a central part of this process and the learning of the language of dreams has been the gift of several teachers who have blessed and guided me. Likewise, I was restored by other cultures, spiritual traditions, medicine ways and the beauty of nature – all these attended to my healing.

It is my hope that this testimony contributes as well to the collective healing required after war – by giving voice to the voiceless, exposing structures that perpetrate violence and advocating for processes of personal and collective healing, reconciliation and true peace. True peace requires not only personal healing of the victims but also collective acknowledgement of wrongdoing and transformation of cycles and structures of abuse. In the 1970s, the efforts of Vietnam veterans to heal and recover from combat exposure focused public attention and raised consciousness in the United States regarding the lasting wounds of war in those whom our country delegates to fight. Healing also requires consciousness-raising about the impact on the populations on whom we make war. It has been suggested that a Truth Commission for the United States would be a constructive way to illuminate our past so that patterns of abuse are not repeated in the future.

In 1995, I returned to the United States after eleven years of work in Nicaragua. I came back because I had nothing left to give. I was dried up and dying inside. The injustice and evil that had been heaped upon the people of Nicaragua in those eleven years had overwhelmed my spirit. The contra war, financed and promoted by my country with a crazed vengeance, had slashed the moorings of my soul and set me adrift in a

desolate wasteland in which I could detect no hope, meaning
or purpose in life.

*I climbed into the silent darkness of solitude and northern
winter, rolling a stone across the mouth of my cave, so no
one, nothing more of the world could come in. I wanted to
shut out all that I had seen during the war. I wanted to sleep
and never wake up. But the stone could not keep the memories out. They seeped in through crevices and welled up from
the earth. They came to me in the cave – memories, faces,
spirits, the dead. There was no escaping them. So I surren-
dered. I listened. I remembered. I cried and, with my tears,
honored all that had been desecrated. They showed me why
I was dying and they told me I was going to have to live again.*

*They showed me that life is a sacred fabric into which we
are all woven. Each of us is a thread inextricably linked to all
others. War rips a gaping hole into this fabric. It cuts deeply
into the being of those who endure or witness it. It also cuts
deeply into those who perpetuate it. War desecrates what is
sacred. The fabric of Nicaragua was virtually torn to shreds
by the violence unleashed on it during those eleven years.
The sacred fabric hangs in tatters.*

*During the decade of the 1980s, my life was woven into
the lives of the Nicaraguans with whom I lived and worked
like a richly entwined braid. The war slashed at this cord,
severing friend after friend. The places where their lives had
been so gently pulled into mine were cut off – ripped away,
leaving ragged, frayed edges.*

*The task for me has been to begin mending – to reach
back into the severed places in myself and reconnect with
what was lost. To gather the loose and gnarled threads and
begin to touch them, run my hands over them, lay them straight
again, generate new strands to attach to what is left of the
old, and slowly mend the holes. Grandmother Spider,[7] mas-*

---

[7] Grandmother Spider is fundamental in many Native American lore traditions and spirituality. She was primary in teaching the Human People about
fire, pottery, weaving and spinning.

ter weaver, who links past and present, showed me how to work like her – to spin new thread out of myself. The future lies inside of us, she says. We must spin out the pain, the grief, the mourning, the anger, the rage, the disillusionment, the despair. Spin it out until a new thread starts to come – clear, strong and healed – a thread with which we can weave anew the sacred fabric.

In 1988, four years after I'd first come to Nicaragua, I was pregnant and could not keep up with the physical demands of my work in the war zones. I spent the year working for the Guatemalan Church in Exile whose offices were in Managua. During that year, as invisible hands knit a child in my womb, I sat in front of a computer translating the testimonies of Guatemalan victims of military repression. Their stories were brutal, grisly and endless. During that year, descriptions of horror beyond belief entered my ears through tapes gathered by priests working clandestinely in the highlands and jungles of Guatemala. Day after day, I strained to hear soft voices, telling unthinkable stories on crude recordings. I rewound the tapes over and over again, careful to catch every word, every detail, and to work their statements onto paper, into English and out into the world.

In retrospect, I realize that the life being spun in my womb provided a balance to the stories of atrocities that were spinning in my head. Grandmother Spider says that this balance must be maintained in order to survive. New thread is spun even as the weaving is being unraveled and destroyed. Guatemalan women know this. In the midst of genocide and exile, the women had one constant request of the international community traveling in and out of Nicaragua during the embargo... Red Thread. They needed Red Thread. Vibrant Mayan Red. The Color of Blood. The Color of Life. Even as their people and culture were being massacred, the women kept asking for one thing. Red Thread. They had to keep weaving.

So I sit at my computer and try to spin and weave. My thread is bloodied and stained, coiled tight inside of me. I pull

To gather the loose and gnarled threads and begin to touch them, run my hands over them, lay them straight again... Grandmother Spider, master weaver, who links past and present, showed me how to work like her – to spin new thread out of myself.

on it gently, coaxing it out. Little by little it comes – memory after memory, face after face – with it comes anger, pain, grief, fear, despair...but above all great love. I have to keep spinning it out. I want to get to the Red Thread.

ONE

A PASSION FOR THE STRUGGLE

Looking back, I can see that ever since I was a little girl I have had a passion for anything that was struggling to live. I was born with this. I was always nursing abandoned kittens, wounded birds, taping together severed earthworms. I would bandage them with utmost care and lay them delicately in cotton-lined boxes for healing.

Almost everything died eventually. Then I would bury each one in a specially selected spot marked with a wooden cross, say some solemn prayers and lay an arrangement of flowers on top. Growing up in the household of a High Church Anglican priest provided me with all of the accoutrements for conducting these rituals – black communion boxes for ministering to the sick, containing glass vials of holy water and oil, incense, crucifixes and a silver paten containing the Blessed Sacrament. My lack of success never deterred me. My need was to tend to them, be with them and care for them, so that they would not be alone in their suffering. I never stopped trying.

I guess it was this same need that pulled me to Nicaragua. On July 19, 1979, 43 years of popular struggle culminated in the overthrow of the Somoza dictatorship. The Sandinista Revolution wanted to give the poor a chance at life. Something new and life giving was struggling to emerge. The United States did not want the change. I wanted to get there to see it alive, before my government killed it.

The same network of churches that was channeling Salvadoran refugees up to the United States for sanctuary[8] began directing U.S. church people down to Nicaragua in response to a call for help from the churches there. The United States was waging war on Nicaraguan communities from its military bases along the Honduran border. Stories of raids, bombings, murders and rape in northern Nicaragua prompted the beginning of what became a steady flow of U.S. church people into the war zones to witness the destructive U.S. forays there. These events were pulling on me like a magnet. I wanted to go. I wanted to see, to witness, to help tell the truth.

In the winter of 1983, I applied to be a long-term team member of Witness for Peace (WFP). The only problem was that they wisely had a minimum age requirement of 22 years and I was only 21. They were considering me anyway. I was praying for a miracle.

In January of 1984, Yvonne Dilling, the Washington, D.C. coordinator of Witness for Peace, told me I was accepted as part of the long-term team. I sensed she was not entirely happy about it. She was a seasoned Central America church worker. She had been with Salvadoran refugees as they were bombed crossing the Río Lempa from El Salvador into Honduras. She hauled children from one bank of the river to the other. Back and forth she swam, under a fire-filled sky, until everyone was ferried across.

Yvonne knew I was green, callow – well-intentioned, but young and naive. She understood what I was headed into.

---

[8] From 1980-1992, civil wars in Guatemala and El Salvador created thousands of refugees, many of whom fled to the United States seeking safe haven. Because the U.S. government at the time did not consider Central Americans to be legitimate refugees, they were not allowed to enter the United States and any person who rendered aid to them here broke U.S. law. Numerous religious organizations throughout the country refused to stop helping Central Americans and publicly offered their churches as sanctuaries for the refugees. Their efforts were known as The Sanctuary Movement.

Yvonne was fighting cancer; that is what it had done to her. It was eating her up. She told me I needed to be in Nicaragua by March. I would turn 22 that month.

→-←

I arrived in Managua on March 15, 1984. The first few weeks were a blur of new sights, faces, sounds, smells and tastes. The one thing that stands out vividly in my memory is that it was mango season. Miranda Collett, a fellow long-termer who was as colorful a personality as the array of tropical fruits in the Oriental Market where we bought the mangoes, declared that we had to eat a minimum of twelve a day while they were in season. At the end of a long hot day of meetings, she and I would sit on the Witness for Peace porch with a pile of mangoes and slurp away at them until we were dripping with the sticky sweet juice. "They'll be gone before you know it," she cautioned, "so we have to indulge to the fullest while we can."

I approached the Nicaraguan revolutionary process with the same exuberance as I did the mangoes. I wanted to take it all in. The orientation process that Witness for Peace had organized for us enabled me to do just that. We learned about the agrarian reform, the literacy crusade, health campaigns, childcare centers, housing projects, food distribution, promotion of culture, art, etc. I couldn't believe what I was seeing. I came home at the end of each day suffused with energy as if a high voltage current was surging through me. To me, this revolution was so charged with life that my body couldn't contain it all. It was too much, too fast, too good.

For me, Nicaragua was the "Magnificat" incarnate. The poor were accorded dignity. The rich were required to share. The landless received land. The illiterate were taught to read. In sign after sign, Nicaragua was Our Lady – growing a savior in her belly – bearing God forth into the world. I was having trouble keeping my feet on the ground. I didn't know if I was walking in heaven or on earth. Sometimes I had to dart into the Witness for Peace bathroom, the only possible place to be alone, to slow down my breathing and pinch myself until nail marks appeared in my skin, to make sure I was not dreaming the whole thing. I started keeping a journal, pouring my excess of energy, images and experiences onto its pages. The journal kept me grounded.

Today the stack of journals that I filled with events and memories are like the nail marks that I dug into in my skin in the bathroom – proof that all I saw was true. As I wrote, I had no idea that within twelve years, the achievements of the revolution would be dismantled and that a former *Somocista*,[9] Arnoldo Alemán, would once again rule in Nicaragua.

In 1983, Fr. Miguel D'Escoto, Maryknoll priest and Minister of the Exterior in the Sandinista government, foretold this to a group of church leaders from the United States when he shared the following words with them:

A revolution is made so that what is there
in a most real manner
can be allowed to grow, and not be suffocated.
It's got to respond very much
to the idiosyncrasy, to the history, to the preferences of
    the people.
And so when they ask me
What is it going to be like exactly?
I say, of course, I've never been pregnant.
But I can think of Our Lady that has a baby in her.
The only thing she knows is that
she is full of life, joy and expectation for the future.
She does not know if it is a boy or a girl,
blonde, brunette or whatever.
She does not know! She does not care! She just wants it
    to be good.

---

[9] A supporter or government official of the Somoza dictatorship.

You NURTURE that life.
You try to eat the appropriate things
and avoid things that will hurt it.
We are full of new life, hope and expectation.

We need more than ever in our history
to be left alone.
This is a time when a country needs to be left alone
so that you are not reacting to external things
and disturbing the course.
What would happen if the lady is pregnant and you set
fire to her house
and she has to RUN for her life?
What if she trips and falls?
What happens if you deprive her of the food she needs
or make her endure other terrible things?
You affect that life.
She will lose the child.

I can't say whether Fr. Miguel realized that his words that day were prophecy – that what he articulated as possibility was in fact a vision of what would come to pass. In the following years, the woman's house was burned, she was starved by embargo, her husband and children were murdered before her eyes, she was raped, and finally she lost the child.

Nicaragua taught me the Book of Revelations. Now I understand the bizarre imagery and titanic struggle. I know what it's like to be pursued by the beast. I saw the woman giving birth to a child with the beast at her loins eager to devour the new life as soon as its tender head emerged from her womb. I was with her. I am a witness to her story.

TWO

A WITNESS FOR PEACE

America had never seen quite such a thing. It is one thing to protest war – it is another thing to move in with the victims.

—Ed Griffin, Witness for Peace

Jalapa, May 1984

After months of anticipation, weeks of orientation in Managua and a ten-hour journey on dirt roads, I have finally arrived in Jalapa, a town on Nicaragua's mountainous northern border. For nearly two years, Jalapa has been the main target of contra raids staged from military bases in neighboring Honduras and as a result, became the first home for Witness for Peace. The house where long-termers are based had been a command post for the *Guardia*[10] during the war of insurrection. Today it is full of people in fluorescent yellow Witness for Peace T-shirts, literature on nonviolence and liberation theology, herbal tea bags and granola bars. Like so many other places and structures in Nicaragua today, this house has been reclaimed to serve life rather than death.

---

[10] Anastasio Somoza's National Guard.

Red Thread

We arrived to find that Jalapa has been on alert for several days due to heavy contra activity in the region. We've spent several days learning our way around town and visiting neighboring cooperatives. The mountains are gorgeous, lush, dripping with life. Yet the threat of attack hovers closely like a shroud, poised to close in and engulf us. I have never felt a place so vibrantly alive and yet so close to death.

In town I watch the women holding their babies tightly against their bodies as Soviet military transport trucks called IFA's race by loaded down with heavily armed Nicaraguan soldiers and I wonder what they feel, what they tell their children, and what they do with their fear? I wonder what possible difference my presence here can make. I want to DO something to overcome the powerlessness of BEing here. I am beginning to see that being a WITNESS does not mean saving anyone. It means simply to be with, accompany, and to tell the story.

Jalapa, June 1, 1984

Word has come that Ocotal, a city several hours south of here, was attacked this morning. We will leave for Ocotal first thing tomorrow morning, assuming the military has opened the road. You don't go anywhere here until the army opens the road. Ambushes and detonating mines are daily occurrences. The army sends patrols to scout out any presence of the *contras*, act as bait for ambushes, and sweep for mines. Mine sweeping is a kamikaze mission consisting of driving slowly on an IFA, while a few *compas*[11] walk along the road poking sticks in puddles and ruts, looking for signs of loose dirt on the road where a mine may have been buried during the night. Throughout this procedure, they are totally exposed and, thus, are like sitting ducks for an ambush or a sharpshooter, not to

---

[11] *Compas – compañeros/as:* literally companion, the "familiar" name given to all Sandinista soldiers.

mention the consequences of stumbling over a mine. This ritual is conducted every morning and, depending on what they find, the road is opened or closed for the day.

There is a somber silence among us tonight as we ready our packs for tomorrow's departure. This is what we have come here for and have been trained to do – to be witnesses to a war that is being carried out by our government in this poor little country of earthen houses and gentle people who grow corn and beans.

Jalapa, June 2, 1984

The next day the road is open and we set out for Ocotal, grateful for the minesweepers. The road winds on and on through the Segovia Mountains. The land is vibrant and alive, emanating an energy we can feel and hear. As we approach Ocotal, however, my revelry in the beauty is abruptly cut short. Here is the war – spread out in front of me. Nothing in the orientation has prepared me for this.

We pull up to the electrical plant that has been blown up and now resembles a grotesque monster of mangled steel. Across the street is the coffee plant, burned to the ground. Everything is still smoldering – piles of burning coffee, the charred body of a truck, a few rifles. The radio station has been bombed, the wood processing plant destroyed and the grain storage silos burnt. People are standing in the ashes sorting through seared grain; salvaging what they can.

We walk through the neighboring homes that have been mortared and are led to a house where a bomb exploded and killed a mother who was trying to evacuate her children. A spray of shrapnel studs the walls of the room where her children had been sleeping. Sun streams into the room through a gaping hole in the mangled sheets of zinc roofing, some pieces of which had dropped onto empty beds and pierced the soft, white, twisted bed sheets. Four children shared that room. Their mother's blood is splattered across the wall.

We then go to the house of the Maryknoll sisters where Sixto Ulloa from CEPAD[12] and Arnold Snyder, WFP Coordinator, are waiting for us. They have driven from Managua with Bianca Jagger[13] and the Red Cross – what a combination! The sisters lead the way to the cemetery where the dead are being buried.

As we approach the cemetery, I hear a multitude of sounds – crying, wailing, and the grating of shovels breaking earth. The place is swarming with people. Graves are being dug everywhere I look. I have to watch my step, careful not to fall into a hole. The holes are like dark, gaping mouths with sweating men standing in them up to their shoulders, tossing out dirt to make room for the dead. Here there is no hiding death under astro-turf as we do at home. Nothing is hidden or left to the imagination.

I stick close to one of the Maryknoll sisters, following her as she makes her way from family to family. I am moved by the way she can reach through this pain and touch the people. She knows them, shares her life with them, has a relationship with them. They don't reject her even though it's her country that has done this to them. They receive her, let her hold them and cry in her arms. I don't have this bond with them. I can't reach out – I can only watch. It is a painful watching. I am so starkly aware of my white skin and nationality. I want to wash it off. But I stand in it, wearing it, surrounded by the human cost of this insane war. I am so ashamed.

I follow Sister across the cemetery to a gravesite where a young woman about my age is writhing in anguish. She is screaming as they lower her husband's body into the ground with ropes. She doesn't want to let go of his body. She reaches for it, lunges after it, and tries to pull it back up out of the hole.

---

[12] Spanish acronym for the Council of Evangelical Churches of Nicaragua, an association of Protestant Churches.
[13] The glamourous, Nicaraguan ex-wife of rock star, Mick Jagger. She was a strong supporter of the Sandinista government.

They restrain her. She is being torn apart as her husband's body is taken away from her. I can't stand to watch anymore. Tears stream down my face. I want to melt into the tree I am standing next to and disappear.

I am now a witness to this war. But at the end of the day, I have no photos, no testimonies, no facts and figures written in my notebook – no documentation. My damn camera has been forgotten all day in the pocket of my pants. I am very quiet. I am ashamed. All I want is to be able to reach through it all and touch the people the way Sister did.

Managua, Later in June 1984

U.S. Senator Jesse Helms and Secretary of State George Schultz were in Managua the day Ocotal was attacked. Their arrival early that morning was unannounced and unprecedented. Around mid-morning, Bob Fretz, from the U.S. Embassy, called Witness for Peace Coordinator, Arnold Snyder, and informed him that Ocotal "had been taken by the *contras.*" He offered Embassy assistance in evacuating Witness for Peace people from the area. Arnold declined the offer, explaining that we were here to stand with the Nicaraguan people and would not be evacuated.

The attack on Ocotal was the heaviest and most well coordinated strike the *contras* had carried out thus far. They had planned carefully and were heavily armed. If they had succeeded in taking Ocotal, news of the "freedom fighters" success (President Reagan's label) would have been all over the U.S. press. Schultz and Helms had arrived that morning and would have been on hand to respond to the *contras* request for U.S. military support in holding "liberated territory."

However, the outcome was not what the Embassy anticipated. The plan failed. Jesse and George left Managua quietly. While Ocotal smoldered, the cemetery filled up with freshly dug graves and people salvaged what they could.

San Juan del Sur, July 3, 1984

For the past year, the *contras'* strategy has been to attempt to take a northern town and position themselves to request direct U.S. intervention. Although these attempts have inflicted great suffering on the people, the *contras* have come up against well-organized popular defense systems and have failed militarily. As a result, they seem to have changed their strategy, seeking other ways to penetrate into Nicaraguan territory. A southern front of *contras*, called ARDE (Democratic Revolutionary Alliance), is now operating along the Costa Rican border, forcing more of Nicaragua's resources and people into defense. In response, our team decided that Witness for Peace will open a new permanent site in San Juan del Sur in southern Nicaragua.

San Juan is a beautiful palm-lined crescent port on the Pacific coast. I will be part of a four-person team based here to document the war on the southern front. The port has been mined and attacked by *contra* "piranhas," high-power speedboats armed with machine guns and mortars. A few months ago, piranhas attacked the port and shot up the fuel tanks that supply the ships. Fortunately, the tanks were empty and fire was avoided. Sadly, there was a casualty when a mother miscarried her unborn child when she went into fear-induced shock during the attack.

San Juan del Sur, Late July 1984

There is a small community of nuns from the Dominican Republic living in San Juan who have been very gracious in introducing us to the Christian Base Communities in the region. In the early 1970's, a Spanish priest, Gaspar García Laviana, served the parish. He, like many other priests in Latin America at the time, fell in love with the people and was deeply moved by their poverty and oppression. His poetry reveals his passion that eventually found expression in the ranks of the Sandinista guerrilla forces, the FSLN, also referred to simply as the Frente.

I felt in my flesh
your poverty
like a whip
of fire.
I wanted to put out
your poverty
with legalistic justice.
It was not possible.
I became a *Guerrillero
Campesino.*[14]
You embraced my entrails
like molten lava
from the breast of the earth;
I want to consume the world
with these ignited verses
that your poverty inspires in me.

–Gaspar García Laviana

Gaspar joined the Sandinista Liberation Front and was killed in combat just before the final successful insurrection against Somoza's dictatorship. He is deeply loved and remembered by the people here. Every year a special mass is celebrated on the anniversary of Gaspar's death. *Campesinos* pour in

---

[14] *Campesino* – a rural peasant, most often a farmer.

from the countryside, filling the church to overflowing. Gaspar loved the poor deeply with a passion that led to his death. He is very much alive in his people today.

San Juan del Sur, Late July 1984

The first delegation I worked with in San Juan was from Pennsylvania, my home state. After picking coffee all day at a plantation to the north, we arrived back in San Juan at dusk with 21 hot, sweaty, dirty, thirsty *gringos*,[15] only to find that there was no water or electricity in town and no idea of when service would be restored. We were also informed that the Nicaraguan border station of Peñas Blancas had been attacked the night before. This news required the group to make a change in plans.

One of the most repeated phrases in Witness for Peace is "go with the flow." This was one of those moments. Everyone rose to the occasion. We guzzled bottles of warm Coca Cola to re-hydrate ourselves and found several creative ways of washing up with no running water. Some settled for the ocean, others swabbed off with "Wet Ones" towelettes and some of us pulled water up from a manhole in the street. I shared one bucket of water with two other women, and like the miracle of "The Loaves and Fishes," we all emerged clean, refreshed and bonded in a way that would never have happened if not for the inconvenience.

The next morning, the delegation went to document the attack at Peñas Blancas. Several months before, the *contras* had launched an attack from Costa Rica and destroyed Nicaragua's border station. In response, Nicaragua constructed a makeshift customs station two miles away from the border – well into Nicaraguan territory and out of firing range. This created a two-mile no man's zone between the Nicaraguan and

---

[15] Term for a foreigner, especially a North American, that depending on the way it's used, can have a scornful or affectionate meaning.

Costa Rican customs stations that must be walked, luggage and all, if one is unfortunate enough to be traveling by local bus.

Our group was permitted to go right up to the chain link fence that divides the two countries and hold a peace vigil on the Pan American Highway where the previous night's attack had occurred. According to the customs officials and border troops whom we interviewed, the Costa Rican border personnel withdrew from their posts shortly before dusk allowing *contra* forces to position themselves along the chain link fence and on the highway to launch their attack. Upon learning this, our group searched for and gathered empty anti-tank launchers and ammunition shells left from the previous night's attack, all bearing the MADE IN USA labels, to take back with them to their senators and representatives as evidence of U.S. support for the *contras*. I felt immensely proud of these folks as I imagined them negotiating their way through U.S. customs in Miami with anti-tank launchers tucked under their arms.

➤◄

Some people speculated that the purpose of the attack on Peñas Blancas was to distract their troops while the *contras* moved onto a *hacienda* on the Costa Rican border from which they could attack the village of Cárdenas on the shores of Lago de Nicaragua, the huge lake in the southwest part of the country. They have repeatedly targeted Cárdenas in the past. We've decided to leave for the embattled village tomorrow. The trip can be made in an hour by car from San Juan, but the road runs along the low-lying lakeshore and is flanked by Costa Rican territory that sits up much higher and from which attacks can be launched easily on vehicles passing below. As a result, the road has been closed for over a year. The alternate route is to leave from Sapoa and travel across the lake to Cárdenas.

If ground transport is a challenge in Nicaragua, water transport is even more so. The Lago de Nicaragua can get very rough with ocean-like waves and contains fresh water sharks that the people fear, although they're small in size and not actually dangerous. The transport craft to Cárdenas is an old wooden fishing boat run by an outboard motor. Parts and fuel for the motor are a constant problem. In addition, Antonio, the boatman, has a drinking problem. As long as he's on the water, he's all right but a trip into town to look for fuel or repair parts can lead to disaster.

We have taken every precaution in anticipation of all potential hazards to transporting a large group of *gringos* to Cárdenas on a very limited time schedule. We have secured fuel from the military, completed all the necessary paperwork to ensure that there will be no hold ups with border officials, made several visits to the lakeshore to assure the boat's availability with Antonio. We've sent food ahead to Cárdenas for the delegation to eat while they're there. Most importantly, we have developed several contingency plans in the event that everything falls through.

Cárdenas, July 1984

We arrived in Sapoa bright and early for a mid-morning departure and were greeted warmly by a *compa* who, after several minutes of acting as if everything was in order, very apologetically explained that the boat had had to make an emergency run to Colón which had been without food for fifteen days. However, the boat was coming back for us if we could wait. So, we waited. In the sweltering heat, we waited – trying to discern if this was a polite, indirect, Nicaraguan way of saying, "The trip is off," and we should take the hint and enact one of our contingency plans – or if the boat was really on its way back. Finally, at about 3:00 in the afternoon, Antonio and his boat appeared on the horizon and we cheered him into shore. By this time everyone was thrilled that the trip was on and so full of Dramamine that the boat's rickety condition didn't even raise an eyebrow.

Fifteen of us climbed eagerly into the boat and, along with our gear, filled it to the brim. We then proceeded to sit for another hour or so while Antonio got something to eat. He had been out on the water most of the night and was exhausted. When Antonio reappeared and, at his direction, 100-pound sacks of beans started to be loaded onboard, I glanced at my co-leader, Mary, who was staring intently over the edge of the boat. She was watching us sink lower and lower into the water with the addition of each sack. So intently was she staring that her glasses slid right off her sweaty face and disappeared into the murky depths. Fortunately, Mary, who is nearly blind without her glasses, also has a great sense of humor. We laughed until our sides ached.

The lake was smooth and we made good time. Three hours later, just as the sun was setting, we approached Cárdenas. Our reception was worth all the waiting in the world. Beautiful children lined the beach – cheering, waving and swimming out to meet us. We unloaded everything in waist-deep water and waded out with our bundles held above our heads. Everyone was there to greet and welcome us.

It's hard to imagine that this little village of 40 some families has been the object of thirteen attacks. After the first attack, people came together and decided to defend themselves and what they had attained in the revolution, in their words, "a future." They say that for the first time in their lives they see a future for themselves. Under the Sandinistas, they have a government that wants them to advance and develop. They now own their land and have a school and a health center. There are literacy classes for the adults. Not wanting to give up what they've gained, they say they are prepared to defend themselves "to the very end." They are fully aware of their vulnerability and of the severity of their situation. Having survived thirteen attacks, this is not rhetoric. Even though bomb shelters and trenches are more substantial than houses, they know the flesh and blood implications of their resolve. Every evening as night falls, they face the possibility of death descending on them from the mountains of Costa Rica. They have every disadvantage militarily but their spirit is high, strong and determined.

The women of AMNLAE[16] prepared an enormous meal for us that they cooked in huge, black, iron cauldrons over wood fires in suffocating heat. After dinner, the delegation invited the community to a vigil for peace. Just as everyone gathered, it began to rain in torrents and the lights went out. Nevertheless, people kept arriving and we had a beautiful vigil that had to be repeated a second time because more people came. At the end of the evening, one of the *gringos* asked the people of Cárdenas what the members of the delegation could do to help them. After a long silence, the response came from an old woman. "We are very poor and isolated. We need many things: food, clothes, books. But our greatest need is that you go back to your country and work for peace. Because only if there's peace, can we build our future which is now in our hands." As she finished saying this, she held up her weathered hands in that dark, crowded room – like a midwife birthing the head of a newborn – and I wondered if she would ever hold the future she longed for.

It had been a long day and we were all physically and emotionally spent. We said good night with many embraces and prepared to go off to our sleeping quarters. On our way out, Diego, the Frente Political Secretary for Cárdenas (the official FSLN representative in town), pulled Mary and me aside and thanked us profusely for bringing the delegation. He was visibly moved by the evening's experience. He said that when we had proposed the idea of bringing a delegation of *cheles,* their slang for "light-skinned people," they had thought we were a bit crazy but after tonight's experience, he was glad that we

---

[16] AMNLAE – *Asociación de Mujeres Nicaragüenses Luisa Amanda Espinoza*, a Sandinista women's organization.

had persevered. "Your country has sent us dictators and marines, war and oppression. I never imagined that I would see what I saw tonight – a boatload of *cheles* arriving in Cárdenas just to touch us, to suffer with us, to accompany us in this struggle. Tonight our peoples touched each other as human beings. Whenever you want to bring people such as these to Cárdenas, they are welcome."

Then his tone sobered as he explained that since the attack of the other night on Peñas Blancas, there had been a lot of contra movement along the Costa Rican border. He confirmed the rumor we'd already heard – that the previous night, the *contras* had moved into a hacienda perched on the hills directly above Cárdenas. He told us that it is owned by a North American, John Hull, and reportedly has an airstrip from which the *contras* have staged previous assaults. He then added that during our vigil earlier, there had been a lot of movement in the *contra* camp and Cárdenas was preparing for an attack. Diego wanted to move our delegation from the church where we had planned to sleep to the emergency health post that was right on the lakeshore, affording an easier escape if necessary. We were to instruct the group to put on dark clothing and move quickly and quietly.

I walked towards the church where the delegation was already bedding down and tried to absorb the reality that these friends – whom I have come to know and love in Cárdenas – will sleep with their children in bomb shelters tonight. How do they explain this to the children? What do the children think of a world in which they must hide in the ground from men who want to kill them at night? The men of the village will watch from trenches all night to protect us. They have lived through this THIRTEEN times. They prepare for it every moment of every day.

We explained the situation to the delegation and they readily agreed to move. Meanwhile, everyone was wearing bright-yellow Witness for Peace T-shirts that practically glowed in the dark, making an inconspicuous move nearly impossible. We did the best we could. Accordingly, a few *compas* took off their camouflage shirts and put them over the shoulders of some in our group as we wound our way through the dark, whispering village of Cárdenas. People were moving in the night, carrying children, taking positions. Everyone had a job to do and some place to be.

We were led to the emergency health post where two medical students from Managua, who were doing their required voluntary service, received us. They were gentle and somber. They had prepared stretchers with crisp, white sheets to receive the wounded and had a pile of freshly folded bandages and a jug of alcohol waiting. They led us to the back of the room where we could arrange ourselves on the floor to sleep. Antonio, our trusty boatman, was trying to rest as well and was prepared to evacuate the wounded in the boat if necessary.

I lay in the dark on the hard ground asking, "Why? Why is this happening? Why are these people being subjected to this? Why should the children of Cárdenas be threatened with massacre tonight?"

I prayed, "Please, God, may nothing happen tonight. Please, God, may the men in those trenches be protected – those men whom I've watched place seed into the earth, pull milk from cows' teats – with their weathered brown hands – the hands that hold guns tonight. Their hands aren't meant for guns. Please protect them, God. And who are these men in the mountains who stalk and kill? What has happened to them? Why do they do this? Why don't You stop them? May morning come soon, God. Bring the morning soon."

➤❬

With the first ray of sunlight, Diego came to rouse us. This was easily accomplished since the tension of imminent attack, an unforgiving concrete floor, heat, humidity, mosquitoes and the assorted noises of 20 people bedded down in one small room with no ventilation – all made for a rather sleepless night.

Diego talked with us while breakfast was being prepared. He has been with the Sandinistas since he was fourteen, initially as a message runner for them during the rebellion. He was caught several times, imprisoned and tortured. The last time, he was tortured so severely that he had to be hospitalized in Costa Rica for several months, during which time the Frente triumphed. After recovering, he was appointed Political Secretary of Cárdenas. Because he has never been to school, the Frente has offered him a scholarship. Nevertheless, he doesn't want to accept because it would take him away from Cárdenas and the people here.

I asked him what motivated him to join the Frente at age fourteen. After a long silence, he asked if I had seen the old well behind the health center. Yes, I had noticed it. "The *Guardia* massacred a group of *campesinos* who'd been working with our beloved Father Gaspar in this region. They stuffed the bodies into that well. My father was one of them," he explained. I looked at him in his fatigues, ammunition vest, black beret, red and black armband with a dagger at his side and wondered how many other fourteen-year-olds had decided to join the Frente because of a dead loved one stuffed into some well.

Before we took off, the group wanted to say their goodbyes to the militia who had slept in the trenches all night. We gathered in a circle – us in our yellow T-shirts, them in rumpled camouflage – all of us bleary-eyed. We communicated our hopes for their safety, peace and future. Either the mood was too somber and needed levity or we were all too giddy from sleep deprivation, but we all ended up dancing the Hokey Pokey in the center of town and having a ball. It was a fitting goodbye.

After many hugs and farewells, we made our way to the lake's edge for departure. The scene that met us was anything but auspicious. The regular motor for Antonio's boat wasn't working. As a result, he was using a frayed shoestring to try to start a little 25 horse power motor he kept on hand. Antonio and his co-pilot had also managed to get a hold of some *cususa,* a local moonshine, with their morning coffee and were a bit tanked up. The sky was dark with rain clouds; the lake was choppy. Conditions couldn't have been much worse. But the group had to get back to Managua to make a flight, so we climbed in.

The lake was so rough that the boat was tossed wildly about and waves swelled over the sides and cut off the motor. Trying to start a motor with a wet, frayed shoestring – in rough water – slightly "looped" – is quite a challenge, but Antonio struggled desparately to get the motor going. The co-pilot had succumbed to the *cususa* and was hanging over the gunwales invoking the aid of every virgin imaginable. He was supposed to be bailing out the boat that was now ankle-deep with water. One of our group pried the bail bucket out of his hands and took over, allowing him to devote full attention to his prayers. It was raining now and the wind whipped at the rain ponchos which people struggled to extract from their soaking-wet backpacks, causing them to smack people in the face and making us look like a wild, yellow sailboat.

I sat there wondering what difference a rain poncho would make since we were already sopping wet and soon to be sub-merged. I was tempted to jump out and swim back to shore before we got too much farther away. I tried not to panic and fall overboard as I watched Antonio rummage furiously through his little box of metallic odds and ends, for who knows what, to start the motor since the shoestring had given out. In the midst of all this chaos, a minister who was seated at the bow of the boat, raised his deep baritone voice and began to lead us in a slow steady chorus of "Swing low, Sweet Chariot." We all joined in and five hours later, we had sung ourselves home, arriving back at Sapoa soaking wet, seasick, but safe. Antonio got a standing ovation and a commitment from the group to raise funds for a new outboard motor.

Managua, November 1984

In November, elections were held in Nicaragua and in the United States. In Nicaragua, the first free elections in 50 years resulted in a clear victory for the Sandinistas. Ronald Reagan won in the United States. I remember listening to the election results on "Voice of America" by candlelight with friends from San Juan del Sur. Mariano, the Political Secretary in San Juan, let his head fall into his hands as I translated the results. "This is a death sentence for us," he said.

Within days of Reagan's reelection, the political fallout erupted in the skies over Managua. Reagan accused Nicaragua of having MIGS, the Russian fighter planes, and gave this as his reason for initiating a major escalation in the war. U.S. Black Hawk jets, performing flyovers, broke the sound barrier with hideous sonic booms meant to send an ominous message to all below. A U.S. destroyer sat off the coast of Corinto in violation of Nicaraguan waters. Nicaragua was digging in, preparing for an invasion.

The long-term team was called to Managua to discern what Witness for Peace should do. The consensus that emerged was to find the most direct way possible to place ourselves between the military apparatus of our country and the Nicaraguan people. Corinto was the place. We decided to form a peace encampment on the beachfront of Corinto and sail out to the destroyer offshore to communicate our intention – that in the event of an attack, we would be on the beach.

Corinto, November 12 & 13, 1984

Twelve available members of the long-term team left for Corinto in a caravan of vehicles. While driving along, we experimented with a new walky-talky system that we hoped would facilitate communication during the planned action. We hung out of the car windows trying to talk on the radios to the next car as we swerved along on the rutted, muddy roads but, in truth, we were doing more yelling than anything else. By the time we arrived in Corinto to present our plan, we were hoarse, wind-burnt and mud-splattered.

In a meeting with the local Frente and some military and state security officials, we explained what we wanted to do. They respectfully sat and listened to this ragtag group of "Don Quixote" *gringos* lay out their plan: "We would like to gather a large group of U.S. citizens in Corinto for a media event in which we would sail out to the U.S. Navy frigate and deliver a message on behalf of the U.S. citizens living in Nicaragua. In a nutshell, the message would say that we are here working with the people of Nicaragua and that we'll be camped out on the beachfront of Corinto until the United States government ceases its threatening behavior. If the U.S. Navy does attack, it will be over our dead bodies."

We also wanted to clarify with the Frente that, although we realized this was a militarized zone and understood that they were responsible for defense, we were committed to nonviolence and therefore could accept no military protection. And lastly, we needed to borrow their tents because we didn't have any.

They agreed to the whole proposal and assigned a couple of unarmed *compas* to find tents for us and to assist us with whatever else we might need. I walked out of the meeting wondering to myself where else in the world could you walk into a war zone during a high state of military alert, propose such a plan and get not only immediate clearance but full support?

Our base of operations became the Baptist church. Pastor Elmer Barahona and his family were tremendously supportive. The Barahonas came from a *campesino* background and were originally from Morra, a mountainous area near the northern town of Jalapa along the Honduran border. Their relatives were early collaborators of Sandino. We literally moved into their house and church.

By the morning of November 12, Corinto was crawling with *gringos* and the press. The Witness for Peace long-term team, delegations from Kentucky and New York, and CUSCLIN, an organization of U.S. citizens living in Nicaragua and opposed to the U.S.-sponsored contra war, had all arrived and we now numbered about 70 people. Things were hectic and the walky-talkies still didn't work right.

We began the action with a prayer service at the Baptist church, incorporating a socio-drama that depicted events going on in Nicaragua. It was a very powerful service and we were glad the press had to sit through the whole thing. Then we proceeded to the docks for a vigil at the site of some burnt fuel tanks and wreckage from the most recent attack by the *contras* that had set the city on fire. Here, we received a disappointing message that there was a problem with the fishing boat we had contracted to take us to the frigate. Apparently, when the cooperative that owned the boat realized that we would be unarmed, they backed out of the deal, claiming that they couldn't risk damage to their boat and their livelihood. We quickly improvised and stuck in a few more speeches to keep things going until word came that a shrimp boat had been found.

It was quite a dramatic moment – to watch us pull away from the dock and head into the setting sun toward the destroyer. Suddenly, to our great dismay, a heavily armed Nicaraguan Coast Guard boat pulled up alongside of us. It took a bit of negotiating – that is, yelling back and forth between boats over roaring engines – to persuade them that we really needed to go alone since this was a non-violent, unarmed action. The press had also gotten hold of a boat and were running along the opposite side of us with cameramen from every major newsgroup filming the whole exchange. Finally, the Coast Guard cutter dropped away. Eventually, the press boat fell behind as well and we continued on alone.

I was beginning to think we wouldn't find the destroyer when the captain spotted it up ahead. Our engines slowed as we approached it. It was enormous, black, still, silent, with no evident sign of life. The only movement was a huge radar dish that slowly circled round and round. Our captain shut off the engine. The silence was eerie. We seemed so pathetically small – like David and Goliath. Stuart Taylor, a Presbyterian minister on board our boat, went to the bow and read our message over a bullhorn in his thick Southern drawl. There was no response – NOTHING – just a massive black hulk of a ship sitting on water and the whirring of a radar dish. It was truly uncanny – since there appeared to be nothing human on board – that without a word or wave in response, the destroyer started up its engines and turned out to sea. We watched it go until it was out of sight and then headed back to Corinto.

Corinto, November 18, 1984

Camp life on the beach is a challenge. Between staying hydrated, attending to visitors and briefing the press, we have our hands full. One long-termer calculated that we average 30 to 40 visitors per hour. One typical morning, I recorded that we had visitors from the CDS (Community Defense Organization), the Juventud Sandinista (Sandinista Youth Organization), the Baptist Church, a sewing class, residents from Zone 3 and Zone 7 of the city, and a steady stream of reporters – not to mention the "regulars," the hammock salesman and the everpresent throng of children. Out of necessity, we organized ourselves into two groups in order to spell each other so that we can rest and keep our sanity.

Walking through the streets of Corinto, I sometimes feel as if I've stepped into a scene from Dickens' London – mazes of leaning, twisted wooden shacks winding back through dark alleyways into deeper darkness, murky water swirling right outside people's doorways – pervasive squalor. I can see the ghosts of prostitutes standing in doorways – the trade was widespread here before the revolution. The Frente considers prostitution to be an economic problem and organized the women into production cooperatives, such as sewing and bakery cooperatives, with their own daycare centers. Photos of the women when they were engaged in prostitution line the walls of the co-op. The women say this is part of their reality and it's not to be hidden. It reminds them where they've been and where they are now. They speak without shame.

The revolution is always organizing and encouraging people to solve their problems together rather than being passive victims. Corinto has been attacked five times. During the last attack, the *contras* aimed mortars at the fuel tanks on the docks. When they exploded, it set the town ablaze. Everyone had to evacuate over the only bridge used to enter and leave the city before it could be blown up. Twenty-seven thousand people were evacuated in three hours – that takes organization!

By the following week, the crisis seemed to have passed. The *contras* were striking heavily in other regions and we decided it was time to leave Corinto in order to follow the incursions.

San Juan del Sur, Late November 1984

Back in San Juan, things were very tense. The militia was fully mobilized to defend in the event of an attack. The Political Secretary was visiting in Vietnam to learn more about border defense. Things were especially critical in Cárdenas, Colón and the tiny villages further along the lakeshore bordering with Costa Rica. It seemed, that in order to survive, some people were apparently cooperating with the *contras*. The Frente feared that this cooperation on the part of villagers would enable the *contras* to launch a successful attack on Cárdenas and eventually take the whole strip of land alongside the lake. They decided to evacuate the villages between Cárdenas and Colón – Sapotillo, Las Cañas, and Orosi.

As we arrived in Sapoa, the persons in charge of the evacuation, Donald Ibarra, and a group of young *compas* were just coming in with a boatload of people and their possessions. It was a dark, dreary, rainy day and everyone looked exhausted, wet and filthy. They had been working without sleep for two days and the young *compas* were saying they couldn't go on any longer. They were bringing out everything: people, dismantled housing, firewood, pigs, chickens, dogs. The cattle were being herded over land. The people were being taken to a place called Fátima where they would be resettled on a coffee plantation that had been confiscated under the agrarian reform. There is enough land there for everyone and a large *hacienda* house that will provide shelter until new houses can be built.

We piled into a truck the Frente had provided to take us to Fátima to visit with the evacuees. We were an eclectic group that could probably only be assembled in Nicaragua or the United Nations: three Nicas, three North Americans, two social workers – one Chilean and the other Spanish – a Scottish doctor, a Salvadoran refugee and one German. The German was loaded down with provisions for a German Solidarity Brigade that was building houses in El Pochote. We stopped there first and were greeted by cheering Germans who had not had vegetables or sugar in over a week and were overjoyed at the arrival of new provisions and visitors from the outside world. After a short visit, we headed off for Fátima.

We had been on the road for over an hour and I imagined Fátima to be just a little farther. But it is *muy adentro,* very isolated. The trip was breathtaking, up and down mountains, twisting, turning, green, green, and more green – so much abundant land and not a house or a person to be seen anywhere. We were almost there when the truck got stuck crossing a river so we went the rest of the way on foot. Packs of howler monkeys followed us through the forest overhead, roaring like lions – a wild, primeval sound that ran right down my spinal cord.

Fátima is breathtakingly beautiful. Maribel and María, the social workers, are part of a team that is living with the people in Fátima to help them to orient and organize themselves. They introduced us to the people – who greeted us warmly and spoke frankly about their situation. They miss their homes terribly and their land. "All my children were born on that land," said one woman. "We had yucca and *frijoles,* beans. My daughter stayed behind with her husband and I miss her." The woman's husband sat with his head in his hands.

We drank coffee and listened as people shared their sadness and confusion. One woman cradled in her arms a very young baby that she let me hold. The child's name was Fátima. "Named for this place?" I asked. "No," responded her mother, "named before I knew anything about this place."

After listening for a while, Napoleon, the Salvadoran refugee, walked off alone, looking very sad. I followed to see if he was all right. He said this was hard for him to experience. He was remembering back to when he left his home in El Salvador, thinking it would only be several weeks, never imagining that it would be years with no hope of return in sight. "The opposition will call this forced relocation a violation of human rights," he said, "and to some degree, they're right. But the real violation lies in the 'created' conditions that require their evacuation."

San Juan de Limay, December 3, 1984

The tobacco farming scene in San Juan de Limay, a small town in north-western Nicaragua, is straight out of the "Old South" – hot, humid, muddy, wet, arduous and formidable – except that with the agrarian reform, the people own the land and the tobacco is theirs. Tobacco is crucial to the local economy so the harvest is a high priority. However, they are very short of workers because so many people have been put on active duty for defense since the town has been particularly hard hit by the *contras* in the last few months. In order to save the harvest, the students of the town have volunteered to pick tobacco. They work all day and study at night. Urged on by Julie Buetel, a WFP long-termer who has been working in Limay with some Maryknoll sisters, Witness for Peace is trying to take more delegations there. We've come to lend a hand in the harvest.

As we work together in the fields – our spirits high – everyone is singing and laughing, especially at Carl, a member of our delegation, who is working arrayed in a bright-yellow WFP T-shirt, a black and red bandana, dangly earrings, and black patent leather shoes that are caked with about three inches of mud, resembling some sort of outlandish platform shoes. From time to time, he delights us with a bit of the "Twist" or something from "Grease." I don't have to translate a thing for him; he just does his thing and everyone doubles over with laughter.

After a long day's work, we straggle back to Limay to find that Sister Nancy is burying a man who was killed in Telpaneca. His wife and sister crouch against the cemetery wall – sobbing – a small heap of human pain just clinging to the wall. Our group huddles together composing a prayer to be offered at the burial. The casket passes by carried by four *campesinos.* The man in front has tears streaming down his face.

Sister Nancy leads the blessing of the grave and in closing, asks for our prayer. I translate as it is read, trying to keep my voice strong so everyone can hear. In the prayer, we confess our complicity in the killing and reassert our commitment to transform our nation's violence. My voice is breaking with my heart as we finish.

We wander back to the *ermita,* the sisters' house. With Gabriela, an Irish sister, we reflect on the day's events, the war and the heavy toll it is taking on Limay. The people scarcely get done burying one person when the next one arrives. Where is the time to mourn, grieve and reflect – to heal – when you are constantly besieged by more and more death?

In the midst of our conversation, Tomás, a delegate of the Word, comes in with a telegram. His brother has been killed and he would like to ride back with us to Managua tomorrow to get the body and bring it home.

Sister Gabriela pounds her fist firmly on the table. She speaks defiantly in her thick Irish brogue, "Don't ever get used to this!" she says. "They want us to get used to it – to wear us down with so much killing. Be infuriated by it! NEVER GET USED TO IT!"

La Trinidad, Esteli, December 5, 1984

We took a delegation to the hospital in La Trinidad, just outside of Esteli, where the survivor of a recent ambush was being treated. He is seventeen years old and when the ambush occurred, he was part of a TELCOR team that repaired downed telephone wires. We visited with him and took his testimony. As we were leaving, several doctors came running after us and asked if we couldn't talk to more of the wounded. They led us into a room and pointed over to a young man's bed. His hand was wrapped in a bandage that was stained with black blood.

"How are you?" I asked.

"Okay," he responded. I sat down on his bed, held his arm and we started talking.

"I was near Murra with my company and the *contras* attacked. It was part of an offensive. I took a bullet in my hand and three in the other arm. The arm got infected and when I got here to the hospital, they had to cut it off." I hadn't even noticed he was missing his other arm. It shook me up. I felt faint and weak. Herman is only 22 years old. His whole body was shaking from head to toe, thumping against the bed. There was a bad smell, decomposing flesh. "It hurts me and I miss it. I miss it," he cried.

Red Thread

The mother of the TELCOR survivor had come with us and suddenly started yelling loudly, "All of Nicaragua is going to be like him – without arms, without legs, without eyes, without noses." She threw her head back and laughed a sick, crazy cackle. She had seen too much of this and it had gotten to her soul.

The doctors lead us to another amputee. "The helicopter couldn't get in to pull out the wounded so I was carried out on a stretcher, along with the dead; it took three days on foot. When I got here there were only bits of my arm left. It was infested with maggots. They had to cut it off. The *contras* had told me to surrender. 'Surrender your mother!' I told them. I've still got this other arm to continue forward with." And then he raised his one arm up and made a clenched fist showing his defiance and commitment to struggle.

Witness for Peace Office, Managua, December 6, 1984

I am in Managua to meet a delegation that arrives tomorrow. Tonight everyone is asleep early. It is so peaceful and richly quiet. I am enjoying a rare moment of solitude. Just then the phone rings and it's Larry, another long term team member, calling in a report. I take down all the details and then read it back to him to make sure I've gotten it all right – 22 people dead, bayoneted and burned, some shot in the head. The phone line goes dead before I can finish repeating his words.

The peace of the night is broken – wrecked by Larry's phone call. More and more heartbreaking news arrives every day. It never seems to stop. We are now using several short wave radios so that we can report the specifics of the *contras'* assaults more quickly. A hotline has been set up in Washington to get the news out rapidly to our North American constituency. But the fatalities keep accumulating faster and faster.

I walk out into the night to get away from it all. Desperately, almost hysterically, I climb the hill behind the WFP house, trying unsuccessfully to leave all the horror behind. There I sit beneath an immense sky, brilliant with stars, and find no comfort in its silence. The stillness feels like a slap in the face – as if it does not give a damn about what is happening all around. I am angered by its unresponsiveness. I am mad at God.

This has to stop. Why can't You stop it? Enough is enough. How can You just stand there and not DO anything? What kind of God acts like this? How can You be so passive in the face of human suffering? Are You so cold-blooded that You don't feel for those oppressed? Are You powerless? Are You there at all?

There, I've said it. I've uttered my doubt that I've been so reluctant to admit to. Maybe You're not there, God. If You are, You're sure not acting like I'd expect. I want the Exodus story – complete with plagues heaped on Washington, D.C., and the parting of the Red Sea. I want dramatic signs that You are with us. I want intervention from on high. But that's not happening. We're running around like fools down here, filling file cabinets full of documentation about unending atrocities inflicted to punish Nicaraguans for simply defending their vision for a better future – and getting our hearts broken. We haven't stopped anything. We haven't saved anyone. So what's the point?

Washington D.C., March 1985

A proposal to send $27 million dollars in aid to the *contras* was up for vote in Congress. Representative David Bonior (D-MI) had called for a congressional hearing on aid to the *contras* in order to look into accusations of widespread abuse of human rights and the systematic terrorization of the civilian population. Witness for Peace organized the testimony to be presented at the hearing. I came here with a delegation from Philadelphia to lobby the Senators from Pennsylvania, both of whom support *contra* aid.

Our delegation met with Senator Heinz. It was an impressive group: lawyers, clergy, and professors from the prestigious University of Pennsylvania. They made an articulate, even brilliant, well-documented argument against aid to the *contras*. But they got nowhere. Their supplications against the *contras'* policy of terrorizing the civilian population and systematic violation of human rights were deflected by the Senator's cold, steely armor. The man was impenetrable. They were unable to reach anything sensitive, tender... human.

I sat listening in a big, smooth, red leather chair, rubbing my feet on the plush white carpet – the same feet that days before had been covered with the dust of the Nicaraguan *campo*. I remembered walking through the cemetery in Ocotal, through the hospital in La Trinidad... so many places I had been in the last year. Emotionally, I was more present to those spaces in Nicaragua than to Heinz' office.

I was the last to speak. The case had been argued fully. There was nothing left to say. I had no lofty credentials with which to introduce myself. "My name is Jennifer Atlee. I work in the war zones of Nicaragua with the people you are killing." I reached into an envelope on my lap and laid some photos out on the glass top of his mahogany desk – slowly, deliberately, one by one – until the desk was covered with tortured, mangled bodies looking up at him.

He stayed in his chair until I laid the last photo down. The last picture was of Paulina, a little four-year-old, with tears running down her face. One little hand is wrapped tightly around her mother's fingers and her other arm is missing – the only vestige is a little round stub tied off at the end like sausage. She is the victim of a land mine – MADE IN THE USA.

Heinz slammed his chair back, banging into the wall behind him. Although startled, I pursued, "This is it, Senator. This is what you are doing. Their blood is on your hands."

"The *contras* are an instrument," he snapped at me.

"They are a bloody instrument, Senator," I snapped back. "They are a bloody instrument, but I hate those lying Sandinistas, and they must be stopped!" He was on his feet, shoving the pictures back at me. Paulina fluttered to the floor, landing face up on the thick white carpet. I gathered her back into my envelope with the others. The Senator's aides proceeded to escort us out of the office.

The next morning, Heinz voted for $27 million dollars in aid to the *contras*. He knew exactly what he was doing.

Washington D.C., May 1, 1985

Today Reagan imposed an economic and trade blockade on Nicaragua. All Aeronica flights to Miami have been suspended. He declared the blockade from Germany where he was visiting a Nazi SS cemetery. Dressed in prison garb, Holocaust survivors were protesting nearby. Eli Wiesel told Reagan not to go and instructed the president that it was a matter of good and evil.

Washington D.C., August 1986

After working for nearly a year with the Nicaraguan Ministry of Social Welfare (INSSBI), I am living back in Washington and working in the Witness for Peace office. The war against Nicaragua is so intense that several of us who work on Central America organized a gathering to talk and pray about what this is doing to us spiritually. Something started to move in this group. I have no idea where it's going to take us, but we are riding something bigger than all of us.

There were three Vietnam vets and one World War II veteran in the gathering. I had never met a Vietnam vet before. These men were intense, anguished, almost desperate. They said they were seeing Vietnam all over again – the same damn bloody scene – feeling it in their bodies. They can't stand it. Haunted by a ghost, they're in great pain. They feel they have to do something.

Washington D.C., September 15, 1986

VETERANS FAST FOR LIFE – Press Release

Forty Christian denominations in Nicaragua called for a worldwide day of fasting and prayer to bring about an end to the war in Nicaragua. On this day, Brian Willson and Duncan Murphy, two veterans of war, began an open-ended fast, dedicating themselves fully to bringing about this end. They join with fasters George Mizo and Charlie Liteky, two other veterans who began fasting on the Capitol steps on September 1 to stop the war.

"In 1945, I was among those who helped to liberate the concentration camps. At that time I made a vow to prevent those atrocities from ever happening again. Forty years later, I went to Nicaragua and heard the same atrocities from the lips of contra victims."   –Duncan Murphy

"In January and February of this year, I went to Esteli, Nicaragua. When I heard the sounds of fighting, I said to my host-mother, 'I hear my money out there.' We kept hearing fighting. Eleven people were killed while I was there. I vowed to stop the war. "   –Brian Willson

"I told myself I had to go to the source of the oppression and put myself between it and the oppressed. I put my canoe in the stream and then, lo and behold, there were three other canoes in that same stream! I hope that whether we live or die, a movement will rise up and stop this war."
                              –Charlie Liteky

"Once I was willing to risk my life for the destruction of life, why not now sacrifice it for peace? This is not a fast for death, nor for martyrdom, nor for suicide... I have to be here. What the American Government is doing in Nicaragua is not being done in my name!"   –George Mizo

Washington D.C., September 30, 1986

The National Witness for Peace office now doubles as the Veterans' Fast for Life office. We are deluged with calls from across the country and Europe from people who are organizing solidarity actions, vigils, relay fasts, and prayer services in an effort to stop the war. We get sacks of mail. The solidarity crowd on the Capitol steps is growing week by week – most are dressed in black carrying white crosses bearing the names of Nicaraguan victims. The phone never stops ringing. People call to thank the vets for what they are doing and to say they are fasting with them. They plead, "Don't let them die. Tell them we will do all we can for Nicaragua."

Washington D.C., October 1986

I was awakened in my sleep last night by a voice that called to me in a dream, telling me to prepare – to get on my knees for confession. I knelt by my bed in the dark while a stream of memories began to pass before my eyes as if I was watching a slide show – memories from as far back as I can remember – things long forgotten, seemingly minute and inconsequential. On and on, they flashed before me and I asked forgiveness for each instance in which I had spoken harshly, been dishonest or hurt someone intentionally or unintentionally. Then another set of scenes appeared in which I saw and forgave every person or event that had hurt me in the course of my lifetime. When it ended, I felt purged and pure.

Then a finger gently lifted my chin, raising my head so that I looked up into a face of light. "You are my daughter," God said. I saw myself as a little girl climbing up onto the lap of this enormous figure, swathed in white garments, full of light, large bare feet spread wide, firmly planted on a slab of stone. I was at home in this lap. I wanted to curl up and stay there forever. God asked me to look ahead. Before us stretched a battlefield which seemed to extend forever in an endless expanse of carnage, blood and gore. Everything was smoldering and in ruin.

"This, that you see before you, is my body. Go into it and love," the figure enjoined; then the vision ended as abruptly as it began. I tried to grab onto to it – to pull it back into my room. I had questions! But it was gone, irretrievable. I was left kneeling on the wooden floor of my room knowing that I had sat in the lap of God and that I had been charged with going back to Nicaragua – back into the war.

Shortly after arriving in Nicaragua, the author happily takes in her new surroundings.

Children's dining hall in a resettlement camp that was established when attacks by the contras *caused the people to flee their homes.*

Co-op school in resettlement camp.

© Photo by Paul Dix

*Lorenzo Osorio, a refugee in a resettlement camp near
Jalapa. He fought with Sandino in uprising of 1927 (left).*

Tobacco drying sheds burned by contras *in March 1986
near Jalapa. The same band of* contras *kidnapped 27
people nearby (above).*

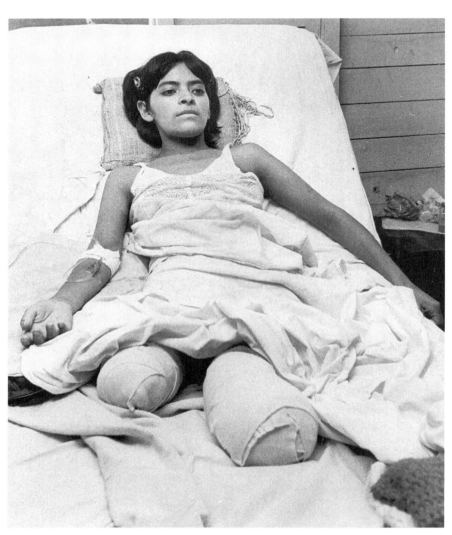

© Photo by Paul Dix

Carmen Marina Picado, 19, victim of contra-placed mine near Jinotega. Six people were killed and 43 were wounded, including 11 amputees.

© Photo by Paul Dix

Non-combative security police killed in contra *ambush near Jinotega on Holy Thursday, 1986, the same day the U.S. Congress voted $100 million in aid to the* contras.

Brian Wilson, veteran, fasting against contra *aid, in Washington, D.C. (above).*

Father Jim Felts leaving Bocana de Paiwas to make his rounds visiting chapels in the war zone (left).

On their way to pick coffee in the early morning, workers receive protection from an armed guard against a contra attack (above).

The author kneeling by María, the mother of Robertito, both mourning the death of that "beautiful little four-year-old" (right).

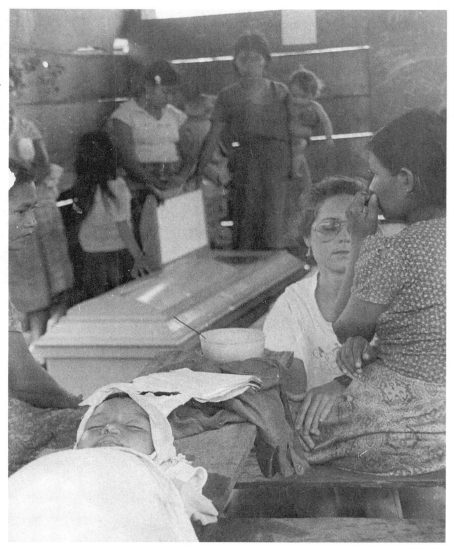

Burial of Carmen Mendieta, 34, who was killed in a contra ambush along with two other women (above).

Geraldin Martínez Galeano, 16, wounded along with her three month old son in a contra attack. A bullet passed through Geraldin's back and stomach and shattered the leg of her baby, Alexei. Geraldin's mother and two brothers were killed in the same attack (right).

Florentina Pérez, wife of José Angel and mother of Zunilda – both killed defending co-op against a contra attack in 1984 (above).

Photo of José Angel Pérez held by two of his daughters (right).

Matagalpa River at Bocana de Paiwas in the early morning.

THREE

CHRIST THE KING PROJECT

Río Blanco, Nicaragua, January 1987

Christ the King Parish covers a sizable area between the Tuma and Matagalpa Rivers located in the center of Nicaragua. It is one of the hottest war zones of the country. Attacks by the *contras* in the early 1980s produced waves of refugees who fled their isolated mountain farms and arrived at the small church in Bocana de Paiwas with little more than the shirts on their backs. The parish priest, Jim Felts, a Marinist from Milwaukee, Wisconsin, worked with the Frente government to develop a plan for resettlement. Under the Agrarian Reform Act, these internal refugees would be given land and a project of integral development, funded by overseas donors, would be created to support them in building their lives again from scratch. The result was fifteen *asentamientos*, or resettlement communities, and Christ the King Project.[17]

I've returned to work in Nicaragua with Christ the King Project. The Project headquarters are in Río Blanco and its office space is set up in a rambling old structure that housed a

---

[17] Christ the King Project was funded by international donors, such as the German Government, Bread for the World Germany, a German Bishops' organization, Save the Children Canada, OXFAM America and others.

brothel in the days of Somoza. This is my new home. Tom Loudon is also working for the Project. He and I first met at the Maryknoll sisters' house in Ocotal where we were both based with Witness for Peace in '84. We became close friends and the relationship has deepened over the years. Tom is my partner and a resourceful mechanic, both of which I need out here.

We are welcomed by Peter Kemmerle and his wife, María Arroyo, also formerly with Witness for Peace. They have been working here for two years and introduce us to the region and the rest of the Project Team: Amparo, the cook – Juan and Chico, the drivers – and Flor and Diana, the social promoters in the *asentamientos*. Not long after, Aynn Setwright, yet one more former WFP long-termer, joins the project.

Due to the *contras'* strategy of assassinating European solidarity workers in an attempt to discourage international support for the Revolution, the Frente has mandated that all foreign nationals be removed from war zones and restricted to areas closer to Managua where they can be protected. I was with the Maryknoll sisters when this plan was first announced and I remember Sister Joan throwing an absolute fit. "There is no way they are kicking me out of here!" she exclaimed, "I'll take to the hills if they try to move me to Managua."

In effect, U.S. citizens are exempt from the mandate. Since the U.S. government has severed diplomatic relations with Nicaragua, imposed an embargo and is financing a war, there is nothing to be lost diplomatically in the event of a U.S. casualty. Ironically, our U.S. citizenship gives us a thin margin of protection to work in the war zones, although ambushes, land mines and psychotic *contras* don't look at passports. One lesson that the United States seems to have learned from Vietnam is that in order to avoid public opposition to a war, you must get proxy forces to do the killing and dying for you. They don't want any Americans coming home in body bags and the *contras* seem to have gotten this message.

Río Blanco developed as a frontier town during the time of Somoza. At that time, this region provided an escape valve for pressure from poor *campesinos* who were being forced off lands along the Pacific coast by the owners of sugar and cotton plantations who wanted to increase their landholdings. Somoza encouraged the *campesinos* to head off for Río Blanco, Bocana de Paiwas and surrounding areas to hack out a space for themselves in the jungle. The town has the feel of the Wild West – complete with pistol-slinging cowboys, saloons and dusty streets.

Travelling east out of Río Blanco, the road branches into four routes that head toward the Atlantic Coast. The road to El Toro is contra territory and closed to travel for us. The *asentamientos*, the resettlement communities, are strung out along the other three roads like islands of the revolution in a sea of contested waters. Our daily activity here depends on navigating those waters that can be calm and safe one moment and treacherous the next. The military has a checkpoint at either end of Río Blanco; they determine if and when we go anywhere.

Tom's work takes him to Managua to round up building supplies, fuel coupons, chain saw and truck parts, do banking, get mail, etc. My work takes me to five *asentamientos* where I work as a social promoter with the communities. This involves accompanying the people, working with them to identify needs and deciding how the project can support them.

The project is funded to build houses, latrines, a school, a health center and a potable water system for each community. The war, however, has made progress very slow. Because these cooperative communities are targets of the *contras*, the first priority is self-defense. Day-to-day survival is such a struggle that the time and people-power required to build decent shelter is hard to find. Many communities are still living in abysmal conditions, squatting under black plastic sheeting in a region where it rains heavily eight months out of the year. Others have managed to put up zinc roofing and then wrap thick, black plastic around for walls.

Red Thread

This year construction plans have been delayed again due to the worsening military situation. The more vulnerable cooperatives are digging miles of circular defense trenches and bomb shelters – rather than putting up housing – so that they stand a better chance of defending themselves when attacked. This is what war demands. It is sad to see them digging trenches day after day instead of building houses. It is outrageous that they have to.

Río Blanco, February 1987

One of the *asentamientos* I have been assigned to work with is called El Achiote. The first time I went there, I didn't actually arrive. Peter said he needed to return to El Achiote to pick up a water technician from Matagalpa whom he'd left off in the morning to do feasibility studies for a water system. Carmen Mendieta, who works with the Project and is from Bocana de Paiwas, and I decided to go along for the ride. The three of us piled into the truck and the *compa* at the military checkpoint waved us on through saying the road was clear.

The road to El Achiote is beautiful. It winds its way through lush jungle and is crisscrossed by rivers and streams flowing down the mountains that rise up on either side. The road twists and turns, wrapping itself around the wild landscape like a tightly coiled snake. We slow to a crawl while making the steep descents into the cool, dark river crossings and find the air full of the pungent fragrance of the white *lirio*, a kind of lily. It is enchanting.

Lost in the beauty around me, I didn't see what Peter observed on the road ahead. Suddenly, the truck lurched to a halt and Peter sat frozen at the wheel. Without saying a word, he opened his door and walked a few feet in front of the truck. I got out on my side and stopped in my tracks. There, on the road, was a dead man. His body was carefully laid out across the width of the road. His face was a mass of red-black blood.

Peter knelt by the man and felt for a pulse. He walked slowly back to the truck and slid into the driver's seat. He recognized the dead man from the cooperative. Whoever did this was close by. If they got their hands on Carmen, they'd do the same to her. We were going to have to leave him, go back to Río Blanco and send the Frente out for him.

Peter turned the truck around in the road. Carmen was hiding on the floor. Just ahead, not 20 yards from the corpse, a man was sitting on the side of the road, watching us. Peter pulled up and idled the truck in front of the man and stared at him. The man met Peter's gaze. They locked eyes for a moment and then Peter drove off.

"He's a *correo,*" Peter said, "someone who collaborates with the *contras*. He was watching to see what we would do."

It was all a test – a sick "marking" of territory. The *contras* don't want us working with the cooperatives. They knew we'd be coming back this afternoon. A man was killed and his corpse strewn across our path – all done to give us a clear message. Out of necessity to not put Carmen's life at risk and afraid of the consequences that the thin line of political neutrality we operate within would be erased, we leave a man's lifeless body on the road, afraid to pick him up and take him home.

This is the ultimate state of powerlessness. This is precisely their goal. It is their coup, our disgrace. We drive home in shock. The beauty that enthralled me moments ago is gone. The contras *pierced it with their murder and it has spun away like a punctured balloon. All that is left is that poor man lying in the dirt and the three of us driving away from him. My ears are ringing as if surrounded by a horde of locusts that grows louder and louder. Death has its day today. The most we can do is stare it in the eye.*

Red Thread

San Andrés, March 1987

Yesterday, we traveled to San Andrés and spent the night. It's another hour and a half beyond El Achiote. Of all the settlements I work with, it is the place I fear the most. It's so remote and so vulnerable. The moment I arrive in San Andrés, all I can think about is getting back out.

The place feels like a trap. A sense of panic descends on me and I begin to imagine all the possible scenarios that could get me stuck here – a problem with the truck, a swollen river due to rain on the mountain, word that the contras *are on the road, circumstances to make the community need us – these thoughts just about paralyze me. I have to make an extraordinary effort to suppress my flight instinct and keep myself functioning in a practical way.*

I cannot imagine living here constantly. I do not know how these women manage to keep sane. There is a haunting dread that they live and move in every moment of their lives. The tension is constant, grueling. There isn't one moment of relief. They live like hunted animals, waiting for the enemy to strike – just waiting. I know that my psyche would not withstand such pressure. It would fragment into a million bits.

I had been dreading the trip for days, praying that the road would be closed. But as luck would have it, the road was clear and the Frente was eager to have us go. They were having us take a generator-powered movie projector and a reel-to-reel film on the life of Carlos Fonseca,[18] to be shown to the cooperative that evening. Their people had left on foot the day before and would be waiting for us in San Andrés. I concealed the film as best I could under the front seat of the truck and spent most of the two and a half hour trip rehearsing how I would talk my way out of this one if the *contras* found that film.

---

[18] Carlos Fonseca was a martyred hero and founder of the FSLN.

We arrived mid-morning and spent a productive day with the cooperative, and the team that is cutting wood for their houses. They have decided to wait until the wood is cut for all 35 houses before beginning construction. As the sun began to set, we tied our hammocks up at the home of the Aruaz family where we would sleep for the night.

The movie drew a large crowd and provided a welcome diversion for the evening. Impassioned speeches were made about the heroism of Fonseca and spirits appeared to be high. When the roar of the generator was cut however, it was evident that other spirits were working that night as well.

From a house on the western edge of the cooperative came the anguished screams of a woman. I was led to the house by several of her friends who explained that the woman has been tormented by bouts of hysteria ever since her husband was killed while doing military service eight months ago. Blanca, they explained, was an evangelical Christian who had been told that her husband was condemned to hell because he died fighting for the Sandinistas.

We entered the house that was lit by a single kerosene wick and gathered around the bed. Several women were physically restraining Blanca's writhing body. Her eyes were locked in an unblinking, zombie-like stare as she screamed unintelligible words at a bloodcurdling pitch. Two words came to my mind as I took in the scene – demons and possession.

The women called her name sharply; trying to break the trance and pull her back from the hell she was in. The women prayed over her for what seemed like hours until she calmed down, came back into herself and cried. We left her sobbing quietly in the arms of her women friends and the silence of the black night.

I climbed into my hammock exhausted and overwhelmed by the evening's events. The rubber boots I was wearing slipped off my feet onto the ground below and I rocked myself to sleep, glad for the fire someone had left burning to cut the chill of the night. It was still dark when I awoke with an urgent need to pee. I reached down for my boots and found that I was totally disoriented. There seemed to be no "down." I discovered I was on the ground, surrounded by warm, hairy bodies and my boots were nowhere to be seen. I was sleeping in a bunch of pigs. Apparently, the pigs had congregated below our hammocks during the night, attracted by the warmth of the fire. My hammock, however, was not well tied and had slipped down the posts as I slept, leaving me nestled in a bed of pigs. I wedged my feet into the tight ball of swine and picked my way out to pee.

I retied my hammock thinking about demons and pigs. I thought about Jesus driving demons into a herd of swine. I thought about what I had seen in Blanca's crazed eyes. I thought about the stacks of little white pamphlets entitled "The Catholic Rite of Exorcism" that I'd always noticed in Fr. Jim's house. I thought about the beautiful human beings who had had their lives stolen from them. I thought about the bloody images of war that invade my sleep and haunt me at night. I thought about the fact that there are spiritual forces at work in this war that I do not understand or feel prepared to deal with.

Río Blanco, April 1987

Doña Vera[19] is a community leader from the cooperative at Wana Wana. The first time I met her, she was tossing a bag full of belongings into the back of our pick-up truck and wanted a ride into Río Blanco. Her plan was to leave the next day with another woman for Puerto Cabezas on the Atlantic Coast. They were going to look for their sons who were on active duty there and spend the rainy season with them. Her husband, Elirio, who is actually her second husband and half her age, and her

---

[19] Don and Doña are terms of respect, especially for elders.

children looked on rather helplessly as Doña Vera climbed into the truck.

Everyone had tried to convince her not to go. She was a key organizer in the community, a historic Frente collaborator, and we needed her in the cooperative. In addition, it was a long, dangerous trip through war zones. She had never been further than Río Blanco and did not know a soul on the Atlantic Coast. To top it all off, her husband was paralyzed on one side of his body due to a bullet wound he suffered when he was in active service. But Doña Vera is a determined woman and no amount of arguing could persuade her to reconsider. She was going to make the trip and that was that. So off we went with Doña Vera.

The next morning, however, she was at the Project waiting for a ride back to the cooperative. Her traveling companion had stood her up and she could not make the trip alone. Doña Vera is a proud, plucky woman and quickly rallied to the new reality. She informed us that since she was going to be here for the rainy season, she wanted to organize the women to plant yucca and plantain. We agreed to support them in whatever way we could and within weeks they had their crops in.

One day we received a note from Doña Vera asking us to attend a meeting of the women's group. Flor and I arrived at the appointed time and after the usual half an hour wait while people trickled in, the meeting commenced. To everyone's consternation, she announced that she intended to resign as leader of the group.

Flor posed several tactful questions in an attempt to find out the reason behind the sudden resignation. Apparently, the whole conflict revolved around a problem of pigs. Several pigs had been entering the communal garden, gorging themselves and damaging the yucca. The group had taken great care to fence the area securely before planting since they previously had had problems with pigs. They had also requested everyone to tie their pigs up rather than letting them run free. Despite their efforts to protect the area, a few persistent pigs were ruining the crops.

One day, Doña Vera took matters into her own hands. She caught the pigs in the garden and cut off their tails in order to identify their owner. As luck would have it, the culprit pigs turned out to belong to her sister-in-law, who lived next door. The sister-in-law was outraged that her pigs' tails were amputated and refused to tie them up. Once again, Doña Vera took action, putting wooden collars on the pigs to prevent them from burrowing under the fence. The sister-in-law didn't like that either. As a result, Doña Vera was relinquishing her job due to the fact that it caused so many people to be angry with her.

After several hours of skillful mediation on Flor's part, the meeting ended with Doña Vera still in the group, the pigs with no tails fastened to a rope and a very rich discussion about what it means to live together.

David Tejada, April 1987

The women in the *asentamiento* "David Tejada" want their houses built as soon as possible. Last year the entire cooperative lived in the *casona*, the large, main house on the property. It's a ramshackle, old wooden building that housed 20 families who somehow found a way to live together without burning the place down.

The people have decided to build concrete "mini-skirts" around the perimeter of their houses in order to have a bullet-proof barrier around them. This requires hauling large amounts of sand and gravel up to the building sites. Dry season is the time to take advantage of the receding rivers that leave the banks of sand exposed. Normally, people have to carry the sand a half-mile straight uphill in five gallon cooking oil cans to get it to the building sites. Flor and I have been trying to facilitate this slow, backbreaking process by using the truck whenever possible. On the days when we are there to help, people are already down at the river's edge by 7:00 a.m. with piled mounds of sand, waiting for us to haul it up. Doña Chepita usually organizes this operation and determines whose sand gets hauled in what order.

But on a particular day, she was nowhere to be found. We loaded up the truck without her and headed for the co-op. I went to look for Chepita while they were unloading and I found her daughter making tortillas. I asked for her mom and a magical, teasing smile broke across her face. Without saying a word, she removed a tortilla from the *comal*, the flat metal pan used to bake tortillas, and took my hand. She led me around the side of the *casona* to a little door that led to what must have been a storage shed at one time. Quietly, she opened the door and pulled me into the little room with her, closing the door behind us.

It was dark inside and it took several minutes for my eyes to adjust from the bright morning sun. She tugged on my hand and we both squatted on the ground. My eyes slowly refocused and allowed me to take in the scene before us. Doña Chepita was kneeling on the ground at the side of a woman who was bare to the waist. A swatch of cloth fell loosely around her waist that was round and taut with pregnancy. She was on her knees supporting herself with her arms that rested on a wooden bench in front of her. She was breathing heavily, groaning softly. Beneath her, on the dirt floor, was a neatly spread square of black plastic – the same black plastic that was given to all the refugees and has become a symbol of their resourcefulness. They make it not only into houses but also cut little squares of it to throw tortillas, transform it into ponchos during rainy season, tuck it in around bare feet in rubber boots to keep the skin from chafing and rotting, and wrap their guns in it to keep them from getting wet and rusted. And here it was again, that black plastic, a drop cloth for birthing.

I recognized Nubia as the woman in intense labor and immediately remembered that her husband had been killed just a month before. This baby, her first, would have no father. Her hair wasn't bound in the tight, shiny braid that she usually wore, but hung in thick, twisted ropes that snaked down her back. Her skin glistened with sweat in the darkness. Her fingers gripped the bench with each contraction and held her steady as a wave of pain and power coursed through her body. Her eyes stared straight ahead – a dark, deep, concentrated stare at something invisible to us but that kept her focused, strong and steady while this power moved through her.

Chepita was one with her, watching every breath, every movement, reading her body. She had her hands between Nubia's legs now, spreading her thighs apart. The contractions were heavier, pounding through Nubia's hips, causing her fingers to dig into the bench even more – every muscle taut. It seemed she was going to shatter, like a machine gone wild. Suddenly Chepita's hands were full of blood. "Nixia, hold her by the arms," she called quickly to her daughter. Nixia grabbed onto Nubia's shoulders and held her steady as her body shook uncontrollably and a mass of glistening black, blue and red life emerged from her body into Chepita's hands.

Nixia had my hand in hers again and was leading me out of the shed. I was transfixed. I had never seen birth before and certainly had not expected to see it this morning. The bright light blinded me and I let Nixia lead me back to the cook fire. She needed to prepare *tibia* for Nubia. This drink, made of toasted corn and cacao, would be Nubia's sustenance for the 30-day period following the birth. Giving birth is called *dar a luz* in Spanish. It means "to bring into the light." What a miracle I had just witnessed! What a blessing! Tears of pride and admiration welled up in me for these women – these incredible women giving birth in a storage shed over a sheet of black plastic …in the middle of a war!

By late afternoon, we'd hauled enough sand and gravel for six families to start building. Things were going so well I hated to call it a day. But nightfall comes so quickly here. There is very little twilight – it's light and then, all of a sudden, it's dark.

We have to be off the road by dark; and I, as the driver, was cutting it close tonight.

I pulled into Río Blanco just after sunset, exhausted and totally filthy. My back was killing me. All I wanted to do was to wash up and get the cement powder out of my hair and skin. I was hoping to God that someone had gone to the river to haul water today. I staggered out of the truck and headed straight for the water barrels at the back of the house praying all the way that there would be just enough to get a little bath.

We were without electricity again and word was we could forget about getting it back again until after the war. A transformer is a rare and precious commodity in embargoed Nicaragua. The *contras* had managed to blow up the last one and there appeared to be no hope of getting a new one. I grabbed my flashlight on the way to the bath stall and had just shined it into the first barrel hoping to find a glimmer of water when a volley of gunfire opened up. It was off in the distance but not very far. It continued for several minutes. All of us at the Project were on our feet.

Within minutes, word came that the *contras* had ambushed a busload of mothers from Managua on the last hill coming into Río Blanco. The bus was a mangled mess and had rolled off the road into a ravine. There was no noise coming from the bus – no one knew if anyone was still alive or not. The Frente wanted to know if we could serve as an ambulance to evacuate any survivors to Matagalpa, the closest city of any size.

Without hesitation, Aynn was ready to go. "Bless her soul," was all I could say. I was so exhausted that the prospect of driving another five hours on hellish, contra-infested roads with a load of dying people completely overwhelmed me. Since I couldn't deal with it, I handed Aynn the keys to the truck and within minutes she was off.

I stood there in the darkness thinking about the scene that lay at the bottom of the hill – a busload of dead or dying humble women, who had never journeyed far from their homes in Managua, lured into these wild mountains by the hope of seeing their sons who'd been away on active duty for years. Their sons would be at Mulukuku and they could spend a day together. They had hoped, for this one day, to see them, to touch them, to assure themselves that they were still alive and, for at least this one day, to feel at peace.

The mothers were all from the same neighborhood in Managua and had been given military clearance to make the journey together. They were each bringing little bundles of homemade favorite foods made of corn and cheese – pinol, rosquillas, cuajada and tamales – for their sons who would eagerly be awaiting their mothers the next day. The young men have been in the mountains for years now – like animals – hunting and being hunted. They have known no comforts. They live in cold, wet fatigues, with rotting feet and "mountain leprosy."[20]

Who is going to tell them that their mothers are all dead and that the contra ambushed them just as they were coming into Río Blanco? Who is going to let them know that this bus full of women and their little bundles of handmade gifts is now a mass carnage lying at the bottom of a ravine?

I should go down to help, but I do not want to face that bus tonight. I don't want to reach into the charred belly of that bus to pull out body parts, groping around for something moving in the midst of blood, skin, bone and flesh. Evil lingers there, and it is powerful. It gets into your mind, under your skin, slips into your soul, especially in the dark. I'm not strong enough for it tonight. It'll get right into me tonight.

There are times I am scared to death. There is part of me that is ready to hightail it out of here – yesterday! But there is another part that has befriended these women who have pitched their tents of black plastic on a little piece of earth. In their quiet, simple way, they have drawn a line in the sand and said, "They have driven me from my home and destroyed

---

[20] Mountain leprosy is a skin disease caused by damp conditions.

everything I had. From here, I am not running." It is a privilege to be with them. That is what makes me stay.

El Achiote, April 29, 1987

In a repeat of the events of three months ago, a second cooperative member has been killed on the road to El Achiote. The road has been closed since the murder and, once again, Julietta, the visiting water technician from Matagalpa, has found herself stranded in the community with no way out. Finally this morning, the military said we could go and pick her up. We bought coffee and sugar for the family of the man who was killed and headed out.

The road is very different for me since my first trip on it. Rather than reveling in the beauty of the jungle, I feel its danger. The road's deep descents into dark pockets of foliage are no longer enchanting – they are traps, perfect cover for an ambush. The *contras* use this luxuriance to their advantage – hiding in it, moving in it, killing in it. It's a sacrilege. They have stolen its sacred mystery and made it into a place of fear. We wind our way on – deeper into the jungle. Our truck flies a yellow and white Vatican flag like a talisman to protect us from harm.

After about an hour, we arrive at El Achiote and pull up in front of a little wooden house on the side of the road. The simple dwelling belongs to Chavela who has graciously accepted her home's role as a way station for anyone passing through El Achiote. Behind her house, the land rises steeply to the settlement at the top of the hill. The ground is all muddy. Julietta has heard the truck approaching in the distance and, as we arrive, she is making her way down the slippery embankment with a huge smile of relief.

Chavela brews some coffee and news begins to swirl around the little wooden house. Diana and I have not been here for more than a week, and there is a lot to catch up on. The cooperative is reeling from the murder of Don Eligio, the man who was killed. Everyone is scared and nervous. They can't get to their fields to pick corn because the men are away on active duty and they can't harvest without armed protection. It has been raining *un cachimbo,* "raining buckets," and the corn will rot if they don't get it in. The trenches are not draining properly and have filled up with water. The scene is dismal.

We climb the hill to the settlement and visit with the family of Don Eligio. The custom here is to keep a period of mourning for nine days. During this time, friends and relatives visit the family and extend their condolences, or *pésame.* On the ninth day, special prayers are offered to end the novena. Diana promises that we will come back and bring candles for the ninth day prayers. We say our goodbyes to the barefoot widow and leave her with her grief and hungry children in her house of sticks and mud. It hurts to walk away and leave her like that. I want to fix it but I can't.

In this reality where so much is shattered and beyond control, the ritual of mourning is protected and kept sacred. Women draw a circle around themselves and hold it – hold fast to that time to mourn and grieve. This one thing is not broken. We are supposed to be building houses and infrastructure in this parish of Christ the King – instead we bring coffee and candles to widows, we step into their sacred circles and help to remember their dead.

✦❖

Julietta is waiting for us at the bottom of the hill, eager to head off. She's a trooper – never complaining once about getting stuck out there. She has found a source that will work for a gravity-fed potable water system and promises to come back with a design and to help install it. For now, though, she is eager to get back to Matagalpa.

No one's prepared for the news that is awaiting us when we arrive back at the Project. We stand there in the doorway with a muddy Julietta and all her gear as Amparo tells us that Ben Linder is dead. The *contras* killed him last night. He was in San José del Bocay checking a water source for output when he was murdered with two Nicaraguans. Julietta collapses in our arms. Like her, he was a water engineer; he was also a close friend.

Ben is the first U.S. citizen to be killed by the *contras*. We feel a gut-wrenching sadness and loss. As I lie down in bed, I have a terrible ache in my stomach and, long into the night, I listen to the sound of Julietta sobbing. We have found a ride that will get her back to Matagalpa early in the morning. They'll bury Ben there tomorrow.

San Andrés, May 14, 1987

The Red Cross woke us early this morning with news that San Andrés was attacked last night. They're leaving within the hour and will come by to pick us up. I make my way back down to my room to get dressed in a state of disbelief.

I'm sitting on the edge of my bed, pulling on jeans, trying to imagine how things could change so drastically from one moment to the next. Diana and I had just been there yesterday afternoon, just a few hours ago. Spirits were high in the community because all of the wood had finally been cut to build the 30 houses. It was all stacked neatly under plastic tarps. We had done an inventory with the *directiva*, the elected leaders of the cooperative, and it was all there... complete... finished. The *motosierristas*, the chainsaw team, packed up camp and came back to Río Blanco with us. Diana and I were supposed to return on Monday to celebrate the beginning of construction.

As I review events in my mind, the sickening realization comes over me that the timing was not a coincidence. The *contras* had been waiting for us to get all the wood cut, stacked and inventoried – so that they could come and burn it all. It was planned perfectly – clearly calculated to send a message that would not be lost on anyone.

I braid my hair tightly. A little bag of animal crackers dangles from my mirror. I'd hung it there so I would remember to take it with me to San Andrés on Monday. The cookies are for Robertito, a plump, beautiful, little four-year old whom I have fallen in love with. His father was killed when the *contras* attacked their village in the mountains and his mother, María, was pregnant with him at the time. I make it a point to visit her and Robertito every time we go to San Andrés. Life is hard enough for folks out there – even harder for a woman on her own. I grab the animal crackers and slip them into my pack.

On the trip out, the Red Cross fills us in on what information they have. Two hundred *contras* attacked at 4:00 a.m. from three different directions. San Andrés had only 40 armed men to defend the settlement. The army never arrived to reinforce them.

We arrive mid-morning and the women crowd around us, holding onto us, telling us what happened. They tell us the *contras* started calling and yelling at them from up in the hills, "Why are you living in this Sandinista *asentamiento*?" They told the women to come to them if they wanted to be spared. A few women started running towards them; most fled to the mountains to hide. The contra fired at them, yelling, "Next time we'll kill you all."

Holding onto each other like a human knot, we stand there, listening, and survey the scene. People have started to improvise lean-to shelters out of scorched zinc sheeting to provide some protection from the sun. Twenty-eight *champas* – simple, temporary shelters – were burnt with all the people's meager belongings inside. The wood for the new houses is now a smoldering pile of ash. This is the second time they have been left with nothing but the shirts on their backs.

We make our way to the school that somehow survived the attack. I step from the bright sunlight into the darkened room. At first I can see nothing, my eyes are still adjusting to the darkness. Then the scene begins to emerge. Five bodies lie draped over planks of charred wood that is supposed to be for their houses. Women and children are gathered around each of them. Adela, a woman from the community, stands at the head of her husband's body; a naked baby on her hip reaches for a lock of his father's hair. Children's hands touch the lifeless bodies that are at their eye level. They touch death, feel it, trying to understand. They are not protected from any of it.

My eyes travel around the room, taking it all in. Then I see María. My eyes stop on her. My gut clenches and I cover my mouth to silence the cry that wells up in me. Robertito is lying on a plank at her side, wrapped in swaddling bandages.

No, my God, not this... not Robertito! Not this little child! I can't stop shaking my head nor stop the tears streaming down my face. He is only four years old. He is the only thing María has left. He's a baby – a beautiful, little, round baby. You DO NOT kill babies!! YOU DO NOT!!! I want to wrap my hands tightly around the neck of the contras *and squeeze this into them... YOU DO NOT KILL!!*

I make my way over to María. She is so still. I kneel down at her feet and lay my hands on her lap. Her stillness seeps into me, quieting me. She says she was running away with him and they shot him in her arms. I stay with her. I listen to each breath she takes – in and out – and each breath of mine. Robertito lies beside us, still. He has no breath. A piece of white cloth fills each nostril. I sit at the foot of the Pieta – María and her crucified son.

This is a trespass. The contras *have hacked deeply into the womb – into a tender, sacred, mysterious place where divine thread is woven into human form. They have thrust themselves into the Holy of Holies with their evil rod. The curtain of the tabernacle is rent in two. From top to bottom, it is torn and hangs in judgement.*

Outside, the scene is too bizarre to believe. The children of San Andrés are scheduled to be vaccinated today. A team from Health Brigades International has transported serum that requires refrigeration in special thermoses, all the way from Matagalpa, and it must be used right away. So mothers are lining up with their traumatized children who now begin to wail from the injections. The line forms through the ashes, wrapping around crates of ammunition and a submachine gun that the army brought in this morning. "What is there left to defend?" I think to myself.

Animal carcasses are rotting in the sun. Everything is in ashes – houses, wood, tools, food, animals, clothing, corn grinders, money, the health care center. It is all smoldering in the brilliant sun.

The Red Cross starts handing out food, cooking pots and clothing. Another line forms and each woman is handed a pot full of clothes. Consistent with the craziness of the rest of the scene, the clothing they're handing out is for a cold, winter climate. Here they are in the tropics – a place of sweltering heat – and they're handing out wool sweaters, coats and flannel nightgowns. I can't believe it. But no one complains. They don't even question. They just take it – a pot of clothes per family. Off they go with their wailing children and quilted bathrobes.

A naked child stands on a scorched patch of earth where his *champa* stood. He digs his little brown feet into the ashes. His eyes glaze over and he rocks from side to side. The rains are coming. There will be no houses. What will they do?

Good God, what have we done to Your creation? I pray for the grace to see beyond the ashes and the killing. I pray for the grace to know that You can heal this damage wrought by human ignorance. I pray for the grace to not be intimidated, to not be afraid. I pray for the grace to believe in You in the face of evil which right now seems much bigger that You. I pray for the strength and grace to be able to sit at the feet of the Pieta and not stop breathing.

San Andrés, May 16, 1987

We return two days after the attack to meet with the people of San Andrés and to see how we can help. They are scared to death. The women want to leave but there is nowhere to go. To make matters worse, one of the co-op members has been gone since the night of the attack. The conclusion is that he was an infiltrator – working with the *contras* the whole time. They are traumatized and feel betrayed.

They met with the army yesterday to request more protection. The army said they can't send troops because they are stretched beyond their limits already. In lieu of reinforcements, they have sent a "spider" – an automatic rifle on a swivel seat. No one knows how to work the thing. It's not what they need.

Our meeting is cut short because we have to quickly leave on an emergency run. Teresa, a woman in the community, had left her baby sleeping in a zinc lean-to while she was washing in the river. Zinc heats up like a microwave in the sun and her daughter had almost roasted by the time she got back to her. The baby is burning up and is badly dehydrated. Diana takes one look at her and says our only hope is to get her to Río Blanco, although she doubts if the baby can even survive the trip.

We leave hurriedly with the frail baby wrapped in blankets and a red woolen hat in this stifling heat. Nicaraguan mothers wrap sick babies up tightly, which in this case, is only serving to overheat the child more. I have no luck in convincing Teresa that the baby would be better off unwrapped. Diana is driving as fast as road conditions will allow but it is taking too long and we are afraid the baby is going to convulse. Diana stops the truck at the next river crossing and looks Teresa straight in the eye. "Your baby is going to die if we don't cut that fever, Teresa. Trust me." Teresa hands over the baby and watches in horror as Diana quickly unwraps her and holds her in the water. The river washes over her little, red, hot body. Then we race her the rest of the way to the health center in Río Blanco – naked and wet – like a newborn. She struggles but keeps breathing. She survives.

Río Blanco, July 18, 1987

Tomorrow, July 19th, is the anniversary of the triumph of the Revolution. There won't be much celebrating here, however. The U.S. Congress is debating another $100 million dollar aid package for the *contras* and they in turn are doing their best to put on a big show to win it. Word has it that their objective is to take Río Blanco on the anniversary date. Things are very tense. All roads are closed. We hear fighting day and night. We keep trying to guess how close the *contras* are, who is being attacked and fearfully wonder what the people in the cooperatives are going through.

Just a little up from the Project, the Frente has pulled a big howitzer onto the main road to do long-range bombing. It is a horrible machine. It catapults bombs that you can hear land several seconds later somewhere way off in the distance. The initial firing rocks the house. Mary Dutcher, also a former WFP long-termer now working for the Project, experienced her first one this afternoon and it dumped her out of her hammock right onto the floor. She looked up at me with a dazed expression that said, "What the hell was that?"

This powerful tool of destruction has a big problem with accuracy. Like many war machines, it's not selective. It just destroys. Unfortunately, there have been some tragic incidents where the bombs have landed on *campesinos* rather than the *contras* they were intended for. Several days after a launch, we might see a bedraggled group of *campesinos* come straggling into Río Blanco, still in shock from the "explosion that came out of the sky" leaving a huge crater where their houses used to be.

I'm glad the machine is there. It is a horrible admission, but the part of me that wants to survive – that does not want to be killed – takes satisfaction in its presence. I understand why the campesinos take up guns to defend themselves. They talk of how they hate it but that it might keep them alive, so they do it. Otherwise, they don't stand a chance.

But what price do I pay when I take up the methods of the killers? What happens in my soul when I am glad that this death machine might keep me alive? What does it mean – when in order to stay alive and continue doing life-giving work – I have to embrace the weapons of destruction, their ways and their means? The powers may not be gaining territory in a geographical sense, but they might be stealing my soul.

Río Blanco, July 20, 1987

Yesterday was the big day, the Eighth Anniversary of the Revolution. The Frente organized a theatrical production, an *acto*, for the afternoon. The place was packed. A few speeches extolling the achievements of the revolution in this zone had been made when the place began to buzz. People were moving in and out whispering to the Frente representatives seated on stage. Suddenly Denis, the Master of Ceremonies, announced a state of emergency and everyone went rushing out of the theater, piling into trucks that were waiting outside. The *contras* had Río Blanco surrounded.

We made our way up the hill to the Project. Amparo, Flor and Nubia gathered their children and followed us. They felt safer at the Project with its cinder block walls than in their homes of zinc sheeting and sticks.

Since health centers were one of the *contras'* main targets, in the event of imminent attack, the health center had to move elsewhere. The Project house was designated as an emergency health post. A team from the health center arrived just after us. We all got busy sweeping and mopping the main room. It seemed sort of ludicrous to worry about a clean floor at a time like this, but it gave us a something to focus on, which was good for our nerves. We readied stretchers with clean sheets and a table with bandages, suture thread, etc. I went around gathering flashlights for everyone. We would be blacked out – no gas lamps, no cigarettes tonight. Any flicker of light could attract fire.

The bombing started about 8:00 p.m. The children huddled under the bunk beds with their mothers. Feeling trapped and helpless under the bed, I found a narrow space between two outside walls. Aynn joined me and we crouched there for hours; our eyes riveted on a sky that lit up like Fourth of July fireworks. Green tracers darted back and forth, followed by explosions and gunfire. The howitzer lunged and roared on its platform in front of the Project.

We were pinned down in the midst of a nightmare from which there was no escape. It made me sick. I pressed myself tightly against the concrete wall and reached for something to hold onto, a way out. I looked up at the stars, shining brilliantly and steadily above – seemingly untouched by the tirade of human idiocy in which we were immersed here below. Protect us, God. Please keep us alive this night, God. Take hold of this beast that is bearing down on us and bind it up. Deliver us from evil.

Río Blanco, A few days later, July 1987

The *contras* failed in their objective to take Río Blanco. However, they did their best to win the $100 million. With the army consumed in the defense of Río Blanco, the *contras* succeeded in attacking San José de Paiwas. The cooperative is a small one and the periphery has been mined by the people to compensate for the lack of armed men. One of the lookouts was found with his throat slit and the *contras* managed to penetrate from that point. They killed eight people – six men, one woman and one child.

As I sit and write this, I am listening to the Voice of America radio broadcast. In his weekly address, President Ronald Reagan makes the statement, "The *contras* are fighting for democracy in Nicaragua and are gaining popularity as people are more informed about the situation."

Well, Mr. President, I wish I could inform you about the situation. I'd walk you around to the back of our little health center to see the pile of dead bodies laid out there – victims of your freedom fighters' escapade for democracy last night. I'd show you the health center staff, the oldest of whom is 25 years old, working in the middle of that pile of carnage, carefully trying to assemble the bodies for burial. I'd show you the young nurse holding a man's arm in her hands and trying to match it with the correct torso. Since there is no running water in the health center because the power lines for the pumps have been cut for months, they're carting water from the river to wash the blood off the bodies that are now attracting swarms of flies. There are only five coffins left in town and there are eight bodies. The *contras* certainly aren't winning any "popularity" around here.

I'd point out the two brothers lying side by side – one with a burned leg and the other with a bloody face, his tongue sticking out and eyes wide open – both with holes in the right sides of their necks. Lastly, Mr. Reagan, I'd show you four-year-old Myra with her soft, little leg broken in half, dangling by a piece of skin where she was shot – a huge swollen hole in her thigh where the bullet exited. Next to her, her mother's guts are falling out of her back. They are still holding onto each other. I would INFORM YOU about all of this.

It seems I have no alternative but to acknowledge the reality of a force of EVIL at work in this world through the actions of some human beings. But this evil has its own very real energy, life, spirit, and power. It has a face, a presence, and makes a sound. I have seen its horrible face in the relentless oppression of the poor and in the tortured, slaughtered bodies of its innocent victims. Its face is terrifying – repulsive. Reflexively, my head turns away – and down – as if in shame; and my whole body draws in on itself – pulls in tight – to ward off, to push away – the heaps of blood and butchered flesh. The evil face laughs as it sees me recoil, repulsed and afraid. It can bear this power down on me as well – transform this human being into a lifeless mass of rotting carnage. It laughs at me in a deranged cacophony of sound because through my fear, I acknowledge its power.

But just at the very moment that it threatens to completely vanquish me, some inner force pulls me into the shiny black/red blood – deep, deep down – to a place where the horror melts away into tenderness. I reach a mysterious depth where I truly see my brother and sister, the sorrowful victims of a brutality of hate and fear. Our eyes meet and join in that pool of blood. Then that damn face of evil can't laugh. I can look into that bloody mass and walk past fear into compassion.

I will not recoil from this evil. I won't cower inside myself as it laughs at me. I will open my eyes wide and clear, and stare straight into it until I reach the life that I know is still there, unable to be destroyed. In so doing, evil's hold on me is weakened. I have seen past its bloody show – the lifeless body, the stench and flies. Evil can destroy life but it cannot create life. My God is Life, and that is the Higher Power with whom I cast my lot. The God of Life has called to me even in the rotting flesh of the victims and shows me a face, a living face, and says that even in this apparent act of utter destruction, "I am here. I am alive. I create. Don't give up, keep walking with me." I take the hand God offers. I am a servant of Life.

FOUR

END OF THE ROAD

Río Blanco, December 2, 1987

Bocana de Paiwas literally sits at the end of the road, at the juncture of the Matagalpa and Paiwas rivers. To proceed on from Paiwas, you go by foot, mule or canoe. It's a Sandinista stronghold and as a result, draws a lot of fire from the *contras*.

Carmen Mendietta is a petite, soft-spoken woman who lives in Paiwas and works for the Project as a social promoter in the settlements there. She is a Sandinista, a community organizer, a Delegate of the Word and the mother of seven children. She has a sharp mind and uses it to advocate for women. She wants to see a day care center in Paiwas so that the mothers can be freed up for part of the day to work on income generating projects. When the Catholic bishop came to Paiwas for a parish visit, she raised the issue of the ordination of women to the priesthood with him. Carmen is an amazing woman. She works to bring life to the poor and the people love her.

Carmen is high on the *contras'* hit list. They want her dead. As a result, whenever we have Project team meetings, our practice is to transport her to Río Blanco in a truck with "Project Christ the King" plastered on the side, flying the Vatican flag and a North American driver with passport in hand. Short of an airlift, that's the best we can do to get her safely to Río Blanco.

Red Thread

Carmen was not supposed to come to the meeting today. We had communicated by radio and decided that since the zone was "hot", she would send in a written report and wait until the next meeting to come in. We would miss her guidance, insights and experience – invaluable to us – but every trip was a risk for her and it seemed best to not take it.

We had just gathered back around the table after a mid-morning break in our meeting when Maritza, the short wave radio operator, burst into the room. I knew that look on her face; I had seen it too many times before – an emergency, an attack, a dead body. I just couldn't believe the next words out of her mouth. "They've killed Carmen," she gasped.

No. Carmen is not dead. Carmen is in Paiwas. It was decided that she was NOT coming to this meeting and she cannot be dead.

But Maritza just kept repeating that Carmen was dead. The *contras* had ambushed the truck she was riding in, killing her and two other women.

This dreaded day – that somehow deep inside we always knew would come – this damn day had come.

Río Blanco, Early December 1987

The next few days are a blur of images and emotions swirling in my mind. I remember the Frente jeep racing up to the Project and a bunch of *compas* jumping out of the back. They are on their way to the site of the ambush and we make plans to meet them there. After replacing a couple of tires that need changing, they pile back into the jeep, which then won't start. After what looks like a Keystone Cops movie take – with people jumping in and out of the jeep, push-starting it, only to have it then lurch to a halt practically dumping everyone through the front windshield – they're finally on their way.

108

We arrive at the site of the ambush just after the *compas.* I slide out of the truck and as my feet hit the ground, I enter that place of suspended time – operating outside of time and space – where all that was REAL a moment ago, becomes a mirage. A ringing sound – like the shrill, piercing call of locusts – permeates the still hot silence of the morning. I've heard that ringing before… when we found the body on the road to El Achiote. It must come when the spirits gather. I can feel them drawing in close to this place – in hushed voices they draw close to witness what humanity has done – to make sacred that which has been desecrated. It is their time and space now – the realm of spirit – and we move in it like ghosts. They help Carmen make this journey that she isn't supposed to make yet. And we pick up the pieces that are left behind.

I hold a piece of Carmen's shattered skull in my hand. Someone else's hand gathers clumps of her hair and teeth. There is a pile of bone and hair belonging to each of the three women. Bombs, guns and mines shatter these lives that are so precious, so sacred. You can't get them back. Carmen is gone forever. She went right out that hole blown in the back of her head and there is no way to get her back.

Father Jim Feltz manages to get to Matagalpa and find Yamilett, Carmen's daughter, before she goes to the coffee harvest. He finds her just as she's climbing onto a truck full of young people – everyone in high spirits – heading off to pick the coffee that the *contras* don't want picked. Fr. Feltz doesn't have to say a word. As soon as Yamilett sees him, she knows. She drops her backpack to the ground and climbs down off the truck. She is going home to bury her mother.

Chanita, Carmen's friend, holds the wake at her house in Paiwas. The house is dark, full of smoke and spirits, and crowded with people crying. Carmen is laid out on a table in the middle of the room, surrounded by flowers. Huge pots of coffee simmer on the fires. Chanita's husband had lain on the same table, in the same smoke and spirit-filled room five years ago. The *contras* had killed him as a lesson to the people. The lesson hadn't been lost on Carmen. She took every precaution. She wasn't looking to die. She was a mother with seven little ones to raise. But she was in love with God – body, mind and soul – and she loved God through the people. She told me once she was scared most of the time. But she said, "We can't let them intimidate us. We are doing nothing wrong. We are doing God's work. They want us to stop but I can't."

The people are singing Carmen's song – the song she loved the most – the song of her soul. The song is strong and as our voices swell with our grief, the song seeps into the smoke and the spirits – rocking us, pulling out the tears, pushing the pain through us. Healing Spirit goes in deep – like a midwife pushing out the afterbirth – wrenching our guts and making our mouths open wide for the pain to come out. It's got to come out – anything left inside will fester and rot. We sing Carmen's song and Spirit works in us so we can let her go:

> I must cry out. I must risk.
> What would become of me if I did not?
> How can I escape you?
> How can I refuse to speak,
> If Your voice is burning inside me?
>
> Before you were formed in the womb of your mother,
> Before you were born, I knew you and consecrated you
> To be My prophet to the nations.
> I chose you.
> You will go where I send you
> And proclaim what I say.
>
> Do not be afraid to risk
> I will be with you.
> Do not be afraid to announce Me,
> I will speak in your mouth.
> I charge you today with My people,

To root out and tear down,
To build up and to plant.

The land is crying out.
It is time to struggle because the people are crying out.
I will be at your side.

          — "Song of Jeremiah," by Gilmer Torres (translation)

Río Blanco, May 1988

    I need to tell Guillermo's story because Guillermo is dead now and that reality is like a gaping hole that has been blasted through the fabric of my psyche, the tattered edges of which are still flapping wildly. Maybe by writing about him, I can tack down the edges; mend this hole a bit so it isn't so ghastly. I finally cried about him last night. I had to make myself do it. I said, "Tom, I've got to cry for Guillermo tonight. I am not going to be hardened to the point where I can't cry." Once I got started, the tears came easily and I sobbed deeply. It is then that I could begin to let go of him.

    Guillermo was the president of the cooperative at Wana Wana – 32 families who left the mountains fleeing the *contras* – and he and his wife, Ilda, and nine children lived in a makeshift wooden house that Flor and I would visit often for meetings and social visits. The co-op, named after Sandino, is the muddiest place I've ever been to. Our four-wheel-drive truck just slips all over the place when we visit and we've learned to abandon it at the top of the hill and walk in to Wana Wana. Once Guillermo had to pull us out with oxen after we'd gotten good and stuck. I have to admit it was the funniest thing I've ever seen. There were a bunch of men trying to push us out but whenever I stepped on the gas, the rear wheels just sent up arches of wet mud. After about a half an hour, we were all drenched in mud from head to toe and couldn't stop laughing at each other. Guillermo took one look at us and went to get the oxen.

Unfortunately, Wana Wana's mud problems extend inside their houses as well as outside. Knee-high rubber boots are a must at all times. The pigs create treacherous wallows that suck the boots right off your feet. Needless to say, it is miserable. Children have to be kept in hammocks or tied to benches to keep them from getting mired in it. People here are still in makeshift housing – whatever they could tack together to form a wall. The priority is to build houses on a higher spot, out of the mud. The cooperative has timber that is being cut now. The problem is that the lumber is about a kilometer into the *monte*, the woods, and with the last torrential rains, access has become impossible. In their last attempt to haul wood, the oxen got mired in chest deep mud. Everyone seems resigned to the fact that they'll have to suspend cutting until things dry out, and that could mean months. They desperately need houses but they are so exhausted from digging miles of defense trenches, doing vigilance 24 hours a day, being on active duty, and trying to eke out an existence, that some folks would just as soon go another year without housing than to try to wrestle the wood out of the mud.

As soon as this was mentioned in a meeting, Guillermo started to squirm, "Maybe we could try lighter loads. Maybe we should try with the other co-op's oxen, they are more experienced. Maybe we could find another route where the mud isn't as deep." Guillermo never gave up. No matter how discouraging things got, he just persisted in his quiet, steady way until he found a way through. Then the others would follow him. The day after that meeting, he was hauling boards out of the *monte,* one by one, on his back.

There are things about him I will never forget – his deep, soft-spoken voice, the way he worked with the oxen, speaking and moving with them, maneuvering such raw power with such gentleness and the little shelf he made to house his precious spiral notebook that contained all his notes and documents pertaining to the cooperative. He had to stand on his tiptoes, on a bench, to reach it. He said it was the only way to keep it safe in a house of mud and nine children.

I remember his large hands. The fingers on one hand were stiff and unbendable because the tendons had been cut by a machete. He struggled to hold a pencil, to saddle his mule, to slip seed into the earth, to hold his gun. His life was a struggle. He approached it all in his quiet, steady way.

I remember the day he invited Flor and me up to the cooperative's lookout. It was the highest point on their land and from there he could show us the full expanse of their holdings. At the top was a command post, manned 24 hours a day. You could see for kilometers. We sat there together in the fading sun, gazing in wonder at the wild land that rolled out below us in every direction. There was a deep silence filled only by the wind that slipped between us, touching our skin like a spirit. From what appeared to be an uncharted expanse of wilderness, Guillermo guided us through the boundaries of the cooperative's land, "From the big *ceiba* tree on that ridge, follow the forest to where it gives way to *milpa*, the corn field. Then go along that ridge to a place where you see bare rock, no vegetation. The stream comes out of the rock and runs right through the middle of our lands. See it? It's lined with *achiotes*."[21] On and on, he guided us through the panorama below. He knew every tree, every creek, every spring (*ojo de agua*) and every contour. I felt honored to be there, to be trusted enough to be shown it all.

The last time I saw him alive, we were celebrating his son's homecoming from military service. Santiago had been on active duty for three years and had just been discharged. Ilda had made an elaborate altar with different pictures of the Virgin Mary, flowers, candles, bits of colored paper, beads, whatever else she could find that was bright, colorful and beautiful

---

[21] Achiotes – Annatto trees. A small tree of tropical America whose seeds are used to make a yellowish-red dye.

to eyes that had seen too much hardship. Prayers and songs were offered and we were all served coffee and *rosquillas*, delicious corn pastries. In addition to Santiago's homecoming, the first cease-fire of the war had been declared. We sat around discussing the implications of the cease-fire with folks from the co-op.

For one thing, they would all be able to come into town for our wedding. Tom and I had decided to get married in Río Blanco. Family and friends were coming from the United States. Everyone at the Project was pitching in to help make it a great celebration. With the cease-fire, we could send the transport trucks to pick up everyone who wanted to come. Guillermo was joking with me and saying that after I got married, we would have to be more formal and he would call me, "Doña Jenny." I told him he'd better not. Guillermo was serene that day.

Two weeks later, just as we returned from our honeymoon in Managua, word came that Guillermo and his son had been kidnapped. Flor and I jumped in the truck and drove to Wana Wana as fast as we could. Evidently, feeling considerable confidence in the cease-fire and excited at the safe return of his son, Guillermo had decided to go see his mother who had stayed in the mountains when the others had fled. He had rarely seen her in the last several years since it was too dangerous for him to leave the cooperative and she was too old to make the journey. It was a fatal mistake. They were kidnapped from her house.

We found Ilda in shock, as was the younger son who had been with his father and brother when they were taken. He had managed to escape and find his way back to the co-op through unfamiliar mountainous terrain.

As soon as the youngest son arrived with word of what had happened, *compas* took off immediately with dogs to track them. They searched for six days. We went to see Ilda every day. Everyday was torture for her – waiting, pacing, dreading, scanning the hillsides for any sign of them. The little son who had escaped was disturbed – he wouldn't eat or talk, he just lay curled up in a ball – locked in the nightmare of seeing his father and brother being taken away. He said Guillermo was begging them to let his son go, "Take me, but leave my son. Please, not my son." That is what eats at me the most. I know that Guillermo could face his own death but not his son's and the guilt of having endangered him.

Late on the afternoon of the seventh day, word came that the *compas* were coming home with the bodies. They sent a runner on ahead to alert the cooperative. They had found them in a deep ravine, covered with brush. The vultures hadn't gotten to them. Flor and I bought coffee, sugar and sweet bread for the wake and Chico, the Project driver, volunteered to drive us to Wana Wana. When we arrived, people were gathering. Cristina, the health promoter, who is all of about fourteen years old, had gotten a small structure of zinc roofing built to house the bodies during the all-night wake and the preparation for burial. The bodies would have begun to decompose and posed a health hazard. They could not be prepared in their own home. Cristina was instructing people regarding health precautions.

It was getting dark and the men had just started a large bonfire when the dogs came running down the hillside. We knew the *compas* were not far behind. I think I was not alone in harboring some crazy, vain, last hope that Guillermo and Santiago were somehow still alive. They would appear on the crest of that ridge and we would cheer them home. The nightmare would be over. This wasn't really happening. But every trace of my innocent Pollyanna hope was smashed to oblivion when the *compas* emerged on that ridge with two hammocks on poles slung over their shoulders. A wail went up from the people as they brought the bodies down. The tension and waiting of the last six days unleashed itself in a raw, primal sound. Ilda shook, cried, dropped to her knees, stood and fell again. Women held her up as she received her husband and son. Everything was swirling in my head – the sounds, the images, the smells, the spirits, the fire.

The poles were laid across some sawhorses. The hammocks sagged down to the ground with their contents. They were tied shut at the top so nothing could be seen. Torches had been lit and the flames cast bizarre shadows on the zinc roofing that housed the dead.

The Frente arrived from Río Blanco with reinforcements to handle defense for the night so that the people could be with their dead. However, there were no coffins left in Río Blanco. The bodies were badly decomposed – they had to be buried before the sun got hot in the morning. Flor overheard a discussion about whose house they could pry *tablas* (boards) off of to make two coffins. That was the straw that broke the camel's back. Guillermo had hauled those planks through the mud, on his back, so that people could have some semblance of a house. No way were they going to dismantle anyone's home for boards for a casket. "Nobody is going to touch those walls. I don't care where the nearest coffin is, we're going to get it," Flor stated with serene yet absolute resolution.

The Frente radioed ahead to Matiguas, a town, an hour away, on the opposite side of Río Blanco. They had coffins there and would wait until we got there. To travel on that road at night was to take your life in your hands. The *contras* had free run of it after dark. I looked at Chico and Flor – they had the most to lose. They didn't have white skin or a U.S. passport as protection. They both had children at home. But without hesitation, they climbed into the truck. I climbed in with them and we were on our way to get Guillermo a coffin.

We pulled up to the guard-post at Río Blanco and handed the person the note from the Frente giving us permission to continue on the road. The *compa* read it and then leaned heavily on the window. "It's *chiva!* Dangerous! Don't stop for anything! You hear me – for nothing! *Que vayan con Dios.* Go with God." He dropped the rope. We flew to Matiguas that night. I don't know how Chico kept the truck on the road. It was the ride of a lifetime.

Someone was waiting for us when we arrived at the Frente office in Matiguas. From there we were led to some sort of military base where we wandered around until we finally came to a little carpentry shack illuminated by a single light bulb. The carpenter had two freshly painted gray caskets waiting for us – one was still a bit wet. We loaded them with care, so as not to mar the fresh paint. We all exchanged thank yous for the various roles we were assuming this night to care for the most recent victims of this horrible war. It was a time of prayer. As we parted, the carpenter couldn't resist his curiosity at the presence of a *chela*, a North American woman, on this night mission. "Where are you from, *compañera*?" he asked gingerly. "From the United States," I answered, dropping my eyes to the ground. The silence was awkward. "But you're not a *gringa*," he countered.

We flew back towards Río Blanco. The *compa* at the rope broke into a huge smile when we pulled up and waved us through on our way back to Wana Wana. A large crowd had gathered by the time we arrived with the coffins. Just when I thought our mission was over for the night, Cristina came over and asked Flor and me if we could help her with the bodies. She had made bandanas from a sheet with which to cover our noses and mouths. We tied bandanas on several *compas* who had volunteered to help as well. Flor and I each held a neatly folded pile of clothing for each of the bodies. The coffins were slid into the shelter along side each of the hammocks. All of my love for Guillermo was in that coffin – that was all I could do for him now, bring him a decent coffin. The hammocks were untied and the edges drawn back. I didn't know if I could face what lay in those hammocks, but there was no backing out now. A stiff, blackened, distorted shell of Guillermo lay curled in the fetal position. His hands had been tied behind his back. A *compa* sliced the rope, freeing his hands. The stench was intense. We had to move quickly. There was no way we could dress them. I didn't even see how they were going to fit in the coffins with their knees bent up the way they were. I peered over my bandana to Cristina for guidance. With the wisdom of her fourteen years, Cristina answered the question I had asked with my eyes, "Each body has its secrets. They'll find their way." Two *compas* lifted each body out of the hammocks and miraculously, each body fit in. We laid the fresh clothes on top of them. Ilda came in for one last look. Then the lids were lowered into place.

Flor and I walked down to the health center with Cristina in the dark. We sat together for a long time without speaking.

It is an honor and a blessing to have been able to serve Guillermo in his death – to minister to the crucified one. Together with the pain and horror of human actions, a tangible sacredness was present and permeated the night. It flowed between the three of us and we sat in the mystery of it with the bonfire burning up on the hill.

In the morning, the community processed with the coffins up to a beautiful, high meadow that had been designated as a cemetery. Blessings were offered at each grave, speeches were made, honoring shots were fired and Guillermo and his son were lowered into the ground. Handful upon handful of earth was tossed into the hole after them – at first, thudding harshly on the wooden lids of the coffins, then growing softer and softer as the blanket of earth deepened.

"They always take the best of us," said Flor as we made our way home.

Río Blanco, June 1988

A kidney infection, that hasn't responded to three rounds of antibiotic treatment, has turned out to be a pregnancy! This is a very welcome sign of new life in the midst of so much loss. It is clear that I cannot keep up with the demands of the work in Río Blanco – neither physically nor emotionally. It is time to go. I will spend several months working with the Guatemalan Church in Exile which has an office in Managua while Tom finishes up in Río Blanco. Then we will head back to the U.S. so that I can explore going to Seminary. I have some serious questions for God, like "Where are you in all of this?" So far, I haven't come up with very satisfactory answers.

Ontario, Canada, January 1989

Owing to the fact that it isn't easy to find someone to do a home birth in the United States if you have just arrived in the country with no prenatal records and no medical insurance, we gratefully accepted Arnold and Linda Snyder's help (WFP Coordinators in 1984) in introducing us to Elsie Cressman, an old order Mennonite midwife in her eighties, who has been delivering babies most of her life. Interviewing me by phone, Elsie asked two questions, "How tall are you and what size shoes do you wear?" Apparently, my measurements met the criteria because she told us to be at Arnold and Linda's one month prior to the due date. Arnold, Linda and their five children have graciously agreed to host the birth.

Ontario, Canada, February 8, 1989

This baby is two weeks late and I am as big as a Volkswagen Beetle. I am literally FULL of life. Yet news from Nicaragua continues to be frighteningly "not full of life." Today we received news that State Security in Río Blanco found a mine that the *contras* had planted, loaded it onto a truck and brought it into town to deactivate. Somehow it exploded in the main plaza, just as school was letting out, killing eight and wounding four. State Security should not have brought it into Río Blanco. Neither should the United States government have given it to the *contras*.

Red Thread

Ronald, George and Oliver,[22] you are the intellectual authors of the crime, and as such, have shown time and again your skill in executive desktop carnage. Will all this be revisited upon you?

Ontario, Canada, February 15, 1989

Today I gave birth to a ten-pound baby girl, at home, with a midwife. I wanted it this way – to give birth myself – no hospitals, no doctors, no anesthesia. I wanted life to come into the world the way it does naturally – with pain, power, danger and joy. Today, I walked in heaven. She is beautiful. Her name is Carmen. The road doesn't end; it becomes a river and flows on.

---

[22] President Ronald Reagan, Vice President George Bush and Lt. Col. Oliver North, the undercover negotiator in the Iran-contra arms deal.

FIVE

FINDING THE GROUND

Colgate Rochester Divinity School
Rochester, New York, February 1990

"Newspaper publisher Violeta Chamorro and her National Opposition Union (UNO) appeared early today to have pulled off a dramatic upset victory over President Daniel Ortega's Sandinista National Liberation Front in general elections marked by massive voter turnout."

"The electoral defeat of Nicaraguan President Daniel Ortega and his Sandinista government signal the end of U.S. involvement in a decade-long civil war that, with its toll of an estimated 30,000 Nicaraguan deaths, became the most bitterly divisive foreign policy issue of the 1980s."

–The Washington Post, February 26 & 27, 1990

Our friend, Jim, called early in the morning and asked if I'd heard the news. I hadn't. He told me to sit down. "The Sandinistas lost the election," he said. I thought he was lying or joking. I couldn't believe it; I went numb. We hadn't even waited up to hear the election results because there was no doubt – none at all – that the Frente would win.

My memory flashbacked to something Flor had whispered to me the last time I was in Río Blanco, "Doña Ilda is not going to vote for the Frente." At the time, the thought disturbed me and I pushed it to the far recesses of my mind. But Ilda was the pulse of the nation and Flor had her finger right on it. Ilda had lost too much – her home, her land, her animals, her husband, her son, her dreams, her hope. Ilda was a widow trying to raise eight children on her own in a house of sticks, in a sea of mud, in a war zone. She had had enough and no one was listening.

Ilda got down on her knees yesterday and cried, "Uncle!"... just like Reagan wanted her to. And who can blame her? Who can ask more of her? Who can tell her she should go on sacrificing and handing over her children to be eaten up by the war machine? Who can tell a mother that her children are better off dead than free? She wants them alive even if it means turning away from the revolution. There were just too many Ildas for a Frente victory.

♦◄

On a summer visit in 1990, the Pérez family, Amancio, Erminia, and their sister-in-law, Florentina, our best friends and adopted family in Nicaragua, expressed to us how they were left reeling from the election results. While listening to the election results on the radio and upon hearing the Chamorro victory announced, Amancio fell onto the bed. He tried to get up but couldn't. He felt seriously ill. Three days he lay in bed. When he could finally stand, he didn't know where to put his feet. He sat on the edge of his bed for another day – not knowing where to go or what to do. The ground was gone from under him.

I was unprepared for Florentina's words when she quietly said, "Jenny, this is the worst thing your government has done to me. This is worse than when I lost my husband and daughter. When they killed José Angel and Zunilda, they took from me personally. It was my individual loss. But now they've taken my people's freedom. They've stolen our hope. They've taken the whole dream away."

Her despair traveled to me and I, likewise, didn't know where to put my feet.

→←

Tom and I had first met Amancio, Ermina and Florentina in 1985 after their co-op had been attacked. We were moved and profoundly impacted by their story and Florentina's in particular.

When Florentina, or Tina as we all call her, was only three, she stumbled into a cauldron of boiling molasses. It burned the skin off her feet and she spent a year in bed with her feet wrapped in gauze. The doctor wanted to amputate one foot because of gangrene. He said her mother would never be able to care for her feet properly in the mountains and she might die. They never went back to that doctor. Tina wanted to walk again.

She still remembers slipping her feet into her first pair of shoes. It was a great sacrifice for her family to buy shoes. But the new skin on her feet was so tender and delicate she couldn't go barefoot. So they bought her a pair of little boots and stuffed them with cotton. She slipped her little feet into the soft cotton and took her first step.

It must have been during that year of convalescence that Tina started dreaming. She couldn't put her feet on the ground, much less play and explore the physical world around her like the other children could. But in the dark silence of her room, she explored the world of spirit and became sensitive to things unseen.

She lost her first son when he was a baby. A doctor said he needed an operation. He gave him too much anesthesia and pushed him back to "the other side." Tina grieved him until she almost died herself. Her husband, José Angel, would find her holding onto his little clothes and crying. She couldn't let go. She wanted to die.

Then she saw him in a dream. He was right there in front of her, beautiful and alive. She lunged toward him and stretched out her hand to caress the roundness of his head. But they started pulling hard from the other side. If she wanted him, she was going to have to go where he was. Spirit was taking her there, pulling hard on her – like a strong river current – and she found herself resisting, struggling against the pull. Spirit said, "Choose, Tina. Live without him or die with him. Choose now." Tina chose life. The grief got easier and she started to heal.

When the struggle to overthrow Somoza began and the guerrillas started moving in the mountains, she knew sooner or later they would visit her. The first night José Angel brought them home, she started feeding them. They would come under cover of night. It got so that she could sense when they were going to come and would have the coffee ready. They would eat, warm themselves by her fire and disappear into the night. Tina hid every trace of evidence. Before daylight, the coffee grounds were buried, cigarette butts collected and burnt, footprints swept off of the dirt yard surrounding the house. No one could track them to Tina's house. She could help them pass unseen.

Zunilda, her oldest daughter, learned her mother's ways. She too had been crippled as a child – polio. She too knew the spirit world. She painted it on the milky-white adobe walls of their house. She gathered clay and discovered an array of pigments to use in her murals. She painted the beauty that she saw in the world around her – trees draped in vines, bright hibiscus blossoms, hummingbirds and the *guardabarranco,* a beautiful native bird with unique tail plumage. One time, she painted a portrait of Sandino because he was an important part of her world. He filled an entire wall, painted all in red and black. She left him there for a while, even though it was dangerous, until word came one day that the *Guardia* were coming through. Zuni grabbed white clay and in seconds, Sandino was gone without a trace.

Tina's family was one of the first to move to the co-op after the triumph of the Revolution. There were no houses yet, so Tina set up camp in the school until they could build. The zone was *chiva* – dangerous! But it was an exciting time and empowering. The land was theirs. The future was full of possibility.

They had only been there several weeks when Tina saw – in a dream – the attack that was coming. She saw the *contras* coming from Las Lajas and surrounding the co-op. She saw where they positioned themselves, where they hid and waited in ambush. She saw the whole thing – in its entirety. People told her it was nerves.

It started at mid-day on December 31, 1985, exactly as she'd dreamt it. The co-op was caught totally off-guard. Most of the men were off working or in town. When the attack started, there were only three armed men in the co-op. On her polio-stiffened legs, Zunilda hurried to the school where her family was encamped, pulled a clean white blouse out of a bag and put it on. She picked up an AKA rifle that she barely knew how to use and walked out. She knew there were over 100 enemy mercenaries out there. She had her mother's "sight." Tina watched her go.

Valentine was assigned by the co-op to evacuate women and children in the event of an attack. He was leading them out the south end of the co-op, the easiest route off the mountain and to safety in Achuapa. All the women and children were following him in a huddled, terrified mass. But Tina had "seen" that the *contras* were waiting in ambush there and she wasn't going. She pulled her children back and veered off to the east towards what is known as *el infierno*, the hellish eastern passage off the mountain that was steep, jagged, wild and dangerous. The other women saw her pull away and they followed.

It took them three hours to make the descent with the children. The concentration required to negotiate each step kept Tina's mind tied down to the immediate terrain in front of her. Her mind couldn't run wildly back up the mountain to see what was being played out above – to imagine who was going to come out alive and who would be dead. She had no time for "seeing" where in the world Juan was. He was her adopted son who was completely paralyzed by polio. Was he able to drag himself to the bomb shelter, pulling himself along the earth like a snake with his useless, withered legs trailing behind him? The descent through hell bought her time – a few precious hours of unknowing.

News came just before dusk. José Angel and Zunilda were both dead. It had only taken a few hours to destroy so much. An ox-drawn cart carrying the bodies was making its way down the mountain. Tina watched it descend, getting closer, wishing she could slow the ox's steps so that the bodies would never really arrive.

She approached the cart as it reached the bottom and wrapped her hands around the wooden poles of its side to steady herself as she looked at her husband and daughter. She ran her fingers over their bodies, talking to them, laying her hands on Zunilda's freshly ironed, white blouse.

Tina was chasing them – searching for them in the spirit world, trying to reach them. But the old ox, Capullo, wouldn't let her go. He shifted the weight of his massive body from side to side, rocking the cart, breaking her spirit journey. José Angel had broken him with a gentleness and respect that had bonded the animal with the man. He was working with Capullo now, one last time, to keep Tina from chasing him and finding him. She needed to stay behind for now, to take care of the little ones, to tell the story so that their deaths would not be in vain.

In the fall of 1986, Witness for Peace brought Tina to tour the United States and tell her story. She came to Washington, D.C. to tell what happened to her village. She spoke to a crowd of hundreds gathered on the National Mall for a rally in support of the Veterans' Fast for Life. Her thick black braids smelled of smoke from her cook fire. She walked slowly, softly past the massive stone buildings of the Capitol – past the corridors of power where decisions were made that burned her village to the ground and destroyed her family. I asked her what she thought of this place. "There are a lot of squirrels," she said. "I like the squirrels."

Back in Nicaragua, José Angel visits her sometimes at night. I can always tell if he's come because Tina is different on those days. Sometimes, she sees him working hard on a mountain. She can see him but there is a distance between them that can't be bridged. On those days, Tina is melancholy – half here and half somewhere else. Other times, she greets me in the morning with the news that José Angel has come to visit during the night. He comes to check on everyone, making the rounds. On those days, Tina is transfigured. On those days, the stone is rolled away, the tomb is empty and death has no power over her.

Tina has seen Zunilda only once, and that was enough. She was making her way up the mountain in the heat of the afternoon and stopped at the house of the midwife, for a drink of water. Tina sat down to rest in the shade of a tree and had almost fallen asleep when she saw Zuni. She looked so beautiful. Zunilda was wearing a skirt and the same white blouse she had on the day she died. Tina called, "Zunilda! What are you doing here? You are so beautiful. How can you be here? I buried you in the ground and that was the end – there is nothing more – that is what we know here."

"Oh, that's a little lie, Mommy," replied Zunilda. "I'm fine. I'm just working really hard. We have so much work to do."

"What are you talking about, Zuni? What work are you doing?" asked Tina in astonishment.

"We are working for the revolution, Mommy." Then she was gone.

Tina felt the solid hardness of the ground beneath her – something concrete – something that would last. She could touch and hold on.

Tina has suffered enough for a lifetime and now, in addition, my country is responsible for destroying her hope. I cannot bear to see her dreams smashed. I don't know what to do. I cannot lobby my congress people about this outrageous effect of U.S. foreign policy – the breaking of a people's spirit and the shattering of their dreams.

This has been the intent all along – "death by a thousand cuts" – to inflict enough individual wounds that eventually the whole body will die. They know that body and spirit are connected. It is the spirit they were pursuing all along. Kill enough bodies – and they killed thousands – and you kill the spirit. It seems to me that this is the most shameful course to take as a country. This is evil. THE U.S. GOVERNMENT HAS DONE EVIL TO NICARAGUA. In naming something as it truly is, there is power. Today this is all the power I have. Tina, José Angel, Zunilda, Gaspar, Guillermo, Ilda, Carmen, Ben, Tom and I ...we are all victims of evil. Tina is terribly right when she insists it is a collective wound – I can neither heal it in her nor heal it in me until it is healed in all of us. But how do you heal from this?

Achuapa, June 1991

The seminary has allowed me to finish my last semester and thesis in Nicaragua. This has enabled us to move to Achuapa so that Tom can work with the Bloque on an irrigation/reforestation project funded by the World Council of Churches. The Bloque is an organization of Christian Base communities that is trying to respond to the needs of the *campesinos* in the zone in an integral way – spiritual and material.

It is good to be back but the reality is a hard one. The achievements of the revolution are being systematically dismantled. I have nearly completed my degree, a Masters in Sacred Theology from Colgate Rochester Divinity School and with these credentials, I should be able to come up with something meaningful to say in the face of this reality.

But I can't.

I have no idea where God is in this dreadful moment in history. All these years we've proclaimed God as liberator in the Misa Campesina. All these years it is what has sustained these humble people and me. Now I cannot speak the words of the Creed without my voice breaking. How can I confess my faith in something that I know not to be true? There has been NO LIBERATION. These people are not free. Someone named it in a base community reflection recently: "God led Israel out of captivity in Egypt. But we didn't make it. We are right back in Pharaoh's hand, trying to make bricks when every day they reduce our quota of straw."

My whole belief in God has fallen apart. The story didn't go the way it was supposed to. I am a theologian and I have nothing to say. My mind and my God have failed me. So I am faced with the dilemma of what in the world to do here. Tom doesn't struggle with this because he's practical, hands on. He plants trees, puts in irrigation systems and gets machinery to work properly. I am an intellectual and I can't figure my way out of this awful moment.

Then the dream came: a woman comes to me and says we are going to a holy place, to the shrine of all that is black. We go down – into the earth – deep into forest – lush jungle – where everything is green and alive – wild – yet ordered. Little rivulets of trickling water crisscross the jungle floor that is covered with moss and moist earth that feels cool and soft on my bare feet. On and on we go – further and deeper into a rich, velvety darkness surrounded by emerald green foliage.

Eventually, the jungle gives way to an earthen-walled tunnel, lined with an elaborate network of roots, some thick and strong, others like fine filigree. We make our way through the earthen tube until it appears to come to a dead-end. An animal hide curtain hangs covering a doorway. We part the curtain and enter a small round chamber with a fire burning in the center. Seated in front of the fire is an ancient, little man. He is a living skeleton. Bones are painted onto his charcoal black skin with white chalk-like powder. He is a good man, safe, to be trusted. I have this "knowing."

I sit down in front of Bone Man. He welcomes me and says he is going to teach me about medicine but we need to get to know each other first. He is very casual, warm and friendly. Suddenly, I see him as a woman. "I am a woman, too," she says. "I just appeared to you as a man because you are so steeped in the tradition that wise people are supposed to be men." The woman is Native American. Her black hair and deerskin dress are richly decorated with white bone beads. She is magnificent. She is numinous – attracting and repelling at the same time. She sits in the middle of piles of bones and skulls – a scene reminiscent of images I have seen of the killing fields of Cambodia.

I am frightened by the bones and draw back. Bone Woman speaks, "Do not fear this place. This place is essential to life – all of life. It is essential to humanity. You are humus, as of the earth. Few make the journey here. I work alone most of the time. I am a creator, a builder. Look at all I create with these bones." Bone Woman makes a sweeping gesture with her arm to reveal an awesome network of terraced, earth structures – running on and on, upward and outward – as far as the eye can see. They are ordered, geometric, pyramid-like constructions of interlaced bone and earth carefully packed together. "These bones that once walked the earth, now create earth – form new earth structures – hold up and regenerate the earth. Nothing is wasted. All is used, even the old, dry bones. I build temples with them, as you can see. Everyone depreciates old bones, but they are like servants. They should be loved. They carry the body around for an entire lifetime and then they hold up the earth. They are always helping. Bones and earth are interrelated."

Bone Woman speaks, "Do not fear this place. This place is essential to life... essential to humanity. You are humus, as of the earth. ...I am a creator, a builder. Look at all I create with these bones."

Red Thread

She continues, "Humans are poisoning the earth with the chemicals of greed and domination. Some humans carry the sickness in their bones. When the bones come to me, I cleanse them. I take the poison out and then with great difficulty, I neutralize it. I smother it with my foot." I see, then, that her foot is badly scarred from contact with the poison. It is not infected, but calloused and burned – the suffering she endures to heal the earth. "I can heal the bones, but I can't stop humans from poisoning the earth. That is the real cure. But the people don't want to work with us anymore. But you must learn and understand the body/earth mystery – the body, life, death, earth, and regeneration of life. This is the medicine your people need." Suddenly she is gone. The Shrine of all that is Black, the earth structures, the bones – are all gone.

I am plunked back into my house in Achuapa in the wilderness of Nicaragua with instructions to learn the body/earth mystery. I have no idea where to begin. But one thing I know, I've touched ground.

Achuapa, July 1991

Within a week of the dream, I found myself in the house of Flor de María, a healer. Flor is a *campesina* woman from Santa Rosa, a tiny mountain hamlet three hours walk from Achuapa. She is living here in Achuapa in order to be more accessible to people. She heals using needles and plants. People here call her, "La de las agujas," the one with the needles. Some say she is a witch.

Flor was attending patients in a room of her house when I arrived. I waited for several hours as people streamed in and out of the pink sheet partitions behind which she works. After everyone had been cared for, Flor herself emerged. She was wearing a beautiful, white cotton dress printed with a bold, brown African design. I had never seen anything like it in Nicaragua. It looked a bit like Bone Woman's dress and I knew I had found my teacher.

I introduced myself and explained that I was interested in studying with her. She looked me over as we chatted casually and then, to my amazement, asked when I could start. The timing was right she said. She was five months pregnant and would need help attending patients once the baby came.

In the weeks that followed, I learned Flor's story. Her knowledge of midwifery had been passed on to her through her mother and grandmother, but her gift as a healer came through her own suffering. As a strong *campesina* woman with unrelenting, arduous responsibilities in her lap – milking eight cows a day, raising four children and studying to be a literacy teacher at night – she paid no attention to the constant ache in her hands that she'd been feeling for some time. But then the pain started to climb up her arms. Within a year, Flor was completely paralyzed. Her husband abandoned her and the children. Flor's mother took them all in. Flor sat on a cot for three years, while her bones stiffened and twisted. Her joints swelled with fluid and raged with pain. Her mother wrapped her in blankets and burned fires under her cot to keep her warm. She was bathed and spoon-fed like a baby.

The doctors said there was no hope. She could live on painkillers but the arthritis was irreversible. Flor wanted to die but couldn't even move her arms so as to cause harm to herself. She told her mother to cut off her waist-length hair because caring for it was a senseless burden. Her mother still has the hair put away in a box – a thick, two-foot-long, black braid – coiled like a snake.

While listening to the radio, Flor heard about Yasu, a Japanese monk who was healing incurables with acupuncture in León. She convinced a Swiss woman working in the region to take her on the five-hour journey to León. This was her only hope. Yasu examined her and said he could help. She stayed in León for one year and returned to Santa Rosa on foot. Flor told Yasu that she needed to learn his medicine for her people. He agreed to teach her.

Achuapa, August 1991

During the week, I help Flor in the clinic as she attends patients. On weekends, she gives me instruction. We sit under the mango tree in front of her house sticking needles into her daughter's baby doll and tracing meridians onto our bodies with an ink pen and transforming ourselves into walking dot-to-dot acupuncture charts. Flor teaches me to see invisible channels, to dowse[23] for energy and to understand plants. She opens a door for me into a world I never imagined existed. She charts a new path for me where my road had come to an end. Each day brings new learning.

The other morning, Flor and I were attending patients in the clinic when Cándida, a woman from town, suddenly rushed in announcing that there was an emergency. Behind her came two men supporting a round little woman who was staggering and moaning in pain. We left our other patients on their beds, pinned down, full of needles, while Cándida explained the woman's situation. She was a *campesina* woman from Monte Frío, a village several hours ride outside of Achuapa. She had been in town buying supplies when her mule threw her. She had badly dislocated her shoulder in the fall.

Cándida had sent for the bonesetter, Doña Amparo, who happened to be in Achuapa today, although she lived in another village. She was on her way but could only reset the arm if Flor would anesthetize the patient with needles. Otherwise, the woman would never be able to withstand the pain of resetting. Flor assessed the situation quickly and sent Griseda, her daughter, off to prepare an herbal tea for swelling and pain. I knew that acupuncture could be used as anesthesia for surgical operations, but as far as I knew, it was a very advanced

---

[23] Dowse – to use a divining rod, such as a forked tree branch, to find underground water. As a diagnostic tool on the body and for the prescribing of medicinal plants, the same method is employed using a copper rod as the conductor that reads the energy vibrations/current inside the body.

form of acupuncture with which Flor had no experience. She, however, was preparing a tray of needles with intense concentration. I reached down to support the woman's arm that was dangling grotesquely in her lap and was surprised to grasp a floppy, fleshy, lower forearm. I looked up at Cándida in surprise. "That was another fall and the bone never grew back together! I keep telling her she is too old to be riding that *malcriado* – she needs to get rid of that nasty mule!" exclaimed Cándida.

By this time, Flor was poised with the needles. She prepared the shoulder with alcohol and inserted the first one, then another. With the second needle in place, the woman's groaning calmed. She began to breathe and to lament the fact that her mule had once again ruined her arm. Flor continued placing several more needles in various points. When she had finished, the pain had diminished noticeably. The woman was able to talk and respond to questions and to ask if anyone had caught her mule so as to prevent it from wandering home without her.

Then the bonesetter arrived. Doña Amparo was a beautiful, old, white-haired woman who had a glow about her. She moved slowly and deliberately, assessing the dislocation. Notwithstanding that it was very bad, she said she could set it. However, she would have to get it absolutely right on the first try, otherwise the pain would be too intense. Doña Amparo positioned herself at the woman's side and laid her hands on her shoulder, feeling and feeling for quite some time. Then her hand grew quiet, resting on the shoulder. Suddenly, with no warning whatsoever, she made a swift jerking motion with her whole body. The patient cried out in pain. Doña Amparo stepped aside and said quietly, "It's done. It went in easily."

Griseda arrived with the woman's tea. She gratefully sipped at the warm brown liquid. I stood incredulous. This woman, who moments before had been crying in agony and looking like a grossly distorted human being, was calmly sipping tea with her arm in place.

Afterward, Flor, Doña Amparo and the woman discussed the advisability of her traveling back to Monte Frío – a rigorous trip – after such an ordeal. They were having little success in convincing her that she should stay in town to rest for a day. "Who is going to feed and water my chickens?" she asked. Fortunately, right about then, a man from Monte Frío arrived who had been on his way into town and had come across the woman's mule headed leisurely back to Monte Frío. He had tracked her down and after discovering what had happened, offered his horse – slow and reliable – to transport her home. He would deal with the mule.

By this time, our other patients were dressed and gathering their bundles to head home. "Just a minute, Mercedes," called Flor. "I have to give you some milk for your conjunctivitis before you leave." This puzzled me because Flor rarely had milk in the house and if she did have such a precious commodity, it was exclusively used for her infant son. Not being able to imagine what she was talking about, I watched as Flor positioned Mercedes on a stool. She unbuttoned several top buttons of her dress, pulled out an engorged breast, tilted Mercedes' head back and squirted breast milk into the infected eye. Mercedes thanked her and said she'd be back tomorrow for more milk.

All of this transpired in the midst of the usual comings and goings of the clinic. It seemed that only I sat in amazement – wanting to stand up and applaud.

Achuapa, November 1991

Some days Flor sees up to 60 patients in the clinic. By mid-morning, the front yard looks like a mule parking lot. People just keep coming and she never turns anyone away. We work in a small, unventilated space with sick people all day and as a result are exposed to a lot of illness. Flor has hung up a sign asking people to please not spit on the floor and we have barred pigs from the house. Both measures have helped improve the hygiene quite a bit. Nevertheless, I find myself constantly fighting some cold, sore throat or cough. Flor says that it's time to start drinking the tea in order to keep up my strength. She's mentioned this tea once or twice before but has never elaborated on it. I was soon to ascertain what she was referring to.

Late one afternoon, an old woman came hobbling in. The odor that exuded from her was enough to make you hold your breath. We got her up on the table and she showed us her feet – the source of the odor. I had never seen feet such as these in my life. They didn't look like feet at all – more like some sort of swollen, moldy, scaly clubs. I am not squeamish and I had seen just about everything come through that clinic, but these feet made me take a step back. Flor, however, was fascinated. She closely examined the woman's feet and asked questions all the while. I couldn't believe how close she got to the stench.

"Florcita," said the old woman, "you are my only hope. I've tried everything. I've spent all my money on medicine from the doctor – and nothing! I've scrubbed them in pine sol; I've soaked them in kerosene. What haven't I tried? Last time I went to the doctor, they were talking about cutting off my feet... so I haven't gone back. You're my only hope, Florcita."

Flor assured the woman that she could help her but the woman was going to have to learn to make a clay mudpack and apply it at home every day. She sent me to bring some clay that we had gathered several days ago. I had never seen Flor heal with clay before so I was fascinated. Flor gathered up the clay and formed it into a bowl shape, handed it to the woman and told her to go out to the latrine and pee into the wet clay bowl. The woman looked up at her without flinching and said, "Then what?"

"Bring it back here," directed Flor.

The woman hobbled off with her clay bowl. Flor started rummaging around in her room and emerged with a sheet of plastic that she spread neatly on the floor. By this time, the woman had returned with her bowl full of pee. Flor directed her to place it on the plastic and knead the pee into the clay. The woman knelt as if before some mystery and started working the liquid into the clay. "Now that is faith," I thought to myself.

Once the urine was worked into the clay, Flor got the woman back up on the table and applied the mixture to her feet. "This will pull the fungus and rot off your feet," explained Flor. We left the woman with her clay pack to dry and went into the kitchen to make some tea. Flor climbed into her hammock as I tended the tea. "Urine is a great healer," she said. "It cured me of my arthritis."

Now, this was the first I'd heard of this and so I said, "I thought acupuncture healed you, Flor?"

"Acupuncture and urine," she asserted. "Yasu taught me to drink my urine every morning. I still drink it when I feel my arthritis flaring up or if I'm getting tired and run down. It gives me energy and protects me from illness. That's why I suggest you start drinking your tea."

"So that's the mystery tea you've been talking about that I need to drink." I had to let that one sink in for a minute.

"I don't tell everyone about this – only those with whom I have a real bond of trust. Some people can't understand it and would think I'm crazy. So I have to be careful whom I prescribe it to – only the gravely ill. That's what cured Doña Chepita of her uterine cancer, just ask her." She proceeded to tell me case after case of people who had been helped dramatically by urine. By the time she was done, she had me convinced.

"Okay, how do you do it?" I asked.

"Well, I have a special little glass that I use only for my tea. I keep it up in that little niche there in the wall. You have to get your first urine of the morning. I squeeze a little orange into it, or you can just take it plain," explained Flor.

We finished our regular tea and went back to check on the woman's feet. Her clay pack was dry and hard. She had fallen asleep and was snoring up a storm. Flor started peeling off the hardened clay and to my amazement, whole patches of rot came off with it, exposing skin underneath. By the time the woman woke up, her feet were "unpacked." She sat up and looked at them in wonder.

In the wake of so much destruction, sorrow and loss, this medicine is a gift – a balm – that penetrates deeply into our pain and restores wholeness. Like tender green shoots of life penetrating into the brick pits of the Pharaoh, it is a sign of hope, of life. We are reconnecting to the earth through this medicine. We take her into our bodies and she heals us. We bathe in her rue and aloe[24] and she cleanses our spirit. She is pulling us towards her, offering herself to us. We are drinking her, bathing in her, making poultices of her, learning her ways again... healing back into her.

Achuapa, July 1992

I see this earth medicine at work in the Bloque as well. With the loss of the election (translate that as "the loss of the revolution"), one of the first things to go has been rural credit for small producers. In our area, banks just closed up and left town. This is devastating for the *campesinos* because they are dependent on credit to put their crops in due to heavy pesticide and herbicide use and when the credit dries up, it's a sure formula for a crisis.

In response, the Bloque has been in the forefront of the push for developing alternative forms of credit. Equally important, the farmers realize they need to reduce their dependency on costly inputs (i.e., chemical fertilizers, pesticides and herbicides). The Bloque has a team of *campesino* agricultural promoters who are teaching the others how to use organic methods – natural alternatives to chemical inputs, alternative crops and how to work with the contour of their land to avoid erosion and runoff.

---

[24] Rue and aloe are medicinal plants used to clear the spirit.

Accordingly, we've brought a visiting Quaker delegation to see the Bloque's training center. One of the promoters, Esteban, leads our group through a field on the property, talking "a mile a minute" – full of passion for this work. Our group can hardly keep up with him as he makes his way from a "windbreak" of Taiwan grass to a special type of super nitrogen fixing bean and on to a plot of lemon grass that serves as insect repellent. It is amazing to see this resurrection of life, hope and energy out of what, not very long ago, seemed like an utterly bleak and dismal situation.

When we come to the end of our tour, one of the women in our group asks Esteban a question, "The Bloque is a Christian organization. What does this center have to do with your faith?" Esteban looked at the woman and without batting an eye stated the obvious, "This IS our faith. Without this, we will dry up and die on this land. This is what is going to keep us alive."

Esteban's words and enthusiasm articulated for me a shift that I perceive in the Bloque – a shift in theological paradigms – from God as liberator to God as giver of life, enfleshed in the earth with whom the *campesinos* are working out a new relationship.

Achuapa, August 1994

My friend Jim is a theologian. He is visiting from the States and wants to talk to Tina. He wants to ask her about the "times." She seems tired and sad but suggests we go to Los Pinos to talk. We make our way to the little pine forest in silence. Tina leads the way to the top of the ridge where we sit looking down over the mountains that roll out below us.

Tina is quiet, serious. She is not talking. I ask her a few questions for Jim and translate her brief answers. Things are bad, very bad she says. So much has been lost. Jim is searching for her thoughts on a way out of this reality – probing Tina for a vein of hope. "No. No. There are no signs of hope," Tina says. "Maybe it is a time of waiting?" suggests Jim. "No. It is a time of sadness," says Tina. There are no more questions. Jim understands that this is all there is to say. This is the way it is – she sees no hope. God has played roughly with Tina and she does not smoothe things over for God.

We make our way down the mountain with a heaviness between us. We stop at the place where Zunilda was killed and rest by the *jícaro* tree that is still scarred with shrapnel. The sun is shining brightly but a strange little gray cloud has gathered right above the *jícaro*. Suddenly, out of a radiantly sunny sky, rain is streaming down on us like silver threads in the sunlight – washing us, wetting us, gracing us. It is pure gift – an embrace from heaven that breaks through our despair and makes us laugh in delight. Tina is smiling and contemplates, "This is a sign of hope. This is holy rain." We run home in it, soaking ourselves in wet, silver threads of hope. A rainbow hangs in the sky over Los Pinos and we stand on sacred ground.

SIX

TOUCHING THE CRYIN' ONES

United States, December 1995

I am home – back in the belly of the beast and what a "mind-trip" it is. I didn't want to come back. But some force has been pulling me for some time now – steady and constant – pulling me back to this place that I never wanted to return to.

I feel as if I have just emerged from a time warp. I've come from a land where my friends grind corn on a stone and don't know how to open the door on a vehicle and have come to a place where dinners are made in a microwave in ten seconds flat and women with designer fingernails, wearing high heels and nylon stockings, drive four-wheel-drive, all-terrain vehicles on well paved roads. I've come from a place where there is never enough of ANYTHING... to Middle America, a place where the supermarkets resemble some sort of theater of the absurd and where families put into a monthly car payment the equivalent of what an entire family would live on for a year in Nicaragua.

But the thing I really can't adjust to is the lie. Here, there was no war. Here, there was no killing, no illegal activity, no lying to Congress. So, life is just fine and dandy. But because my soul is dragging around thousands of dead people, I just can't adjust to this version of reality.

Red Thread

The United States is a consummate learner of the lessons of the Vietnam War – that when you carry out an illegal and morally indefensible war – make sure you get a proxy force to do the killing. Have no body bags come home. No evidence – no fuss, no muss. Run drugs, make arms deals, whatever you want – to get the money to pay someone else to do the killing. The strategy worked well. Here in the States, it's as if nothing ever happened. There are no veterans of the war with Nicaragua and no Memorial Wall. No one has to remember. No one will care.

So what do I do with all these things my eyes have seen – with the thousands of people killed, with the amputees, with the mothers who are still crying in the night for their dead children? What do I do with all these bodies I'm dragging around? They come into rooms with me and make everyone uncomfortable and stain the white carpets of family rooms. We make a mess in these suburban homes. We shatter the neatly framed portrait of America. We know the deep family secret, the lie. Everyone hopes we will keep our mouths shut.

How did this get to be my home? Why was I pulled back here? What am I doing here? Feelings well up and overwhelm me. Memories surface from some mysterious subterranean source, pouring themselves into my days and my nights – my thoughts and my dreams. They come from a place deep inside and exit through my eyes in a river of tears. I sit before a computer and try once again to catch every face, every emotion, every detail – working these water memories – into words, poems, prayers – into one whole piece.

Wayne, Pennsylvania, January 27, 1996

I dreamt of a huge, black woman sitting on a wooden birthing stool. She had bare feet and her legs were stretched wide apart so that her red, gingham skirt hung deeply like a hammock. Her skirt was full of people and she started talking to me:

144

The Cryin' Ones

Come close child and listen to me.
I's so full of the pain of my people
So, so, full
Of all that's gotta change,
Of all the things that happened.
God don't forget
And we ain't movin' till every tear is wiped dry,
Every single tear,
They all count.
The human race ain't movin'
Till we heal and learn to live right.

I got 'em all in my skirt,
All the cryin' ones -
The slavery cryin' ones,
The Holocaust,
Hiroshima,
And Salvador cryin' ones;
The 'Nam
And Nicaragua cryin' ones;
The whole Trail of Tears.
I'm holdin' 'em all in my skirt,
Rockin' 'em slow.
They safe with me; they okay.
But they waitin', waitin'.

The people gotta come touch 'em
And say sorry.
I am so, so sorry
And mean it with all they heart.
And live so it don't never happen again
On the face of this earth.
Now you go
Tell the people to come touch the cryin' ones.

"Ultimate Grace," etching by Judith Anderson, photo by Jim Colando

I's so full of the pain of my people.
...every single tear, they all count.
...Tell the people to come touch the cryin' ones.

Wayne, Pennsylvania, June 1996

I just received a report on Guatemala called "Unearthing the Truth: Exhuming a Decade of Terror in Guatemala" (EPICA/ CHRLA, 1996) As I leaf through its pages, I can hardly believe my eyes. The Truth Commission has determined that in order to lay a foundation for justice in Guatemala, the truth about what was done must be told. So the clandestine mass graves of the victims, mostly indigenous Mayan people, of hundreds of massacres committed by the Guatemalan security forces are being opened up and the skeletons are being identified. The report includes photograph after photograph of bones being pulled up out of the earth. The Guatemalan military stuffed their sins into the earth and now she is yielding them back up – bone by bone. A member of the Guatemalan Forensic Anthropology Team states, "Even if 30 forensic teams worked for 30 years that still wouldn't be enough resources or time to exhume all the mass graves in Guatemala."

I remember the hours of testimony I transcribed, while in Nicaragua, for the Guatemalan Church in Exile in order to provide some record of these atrocities. Never in my wildest imagination, did I ever dream the truth would actually be told – bone by precious bone.

We are touching the cryin' ones. From deep inside of me came words I could not hold back:

Sacrament of Bone

Bone by bone
Skeletons emerge from earth.
Families look on with eyes of compassion
Waiting to receive the sacrament of bone.

Truth opens the grave,
Pulling up skeletons

Red Thread

Bone by bone
From their hiding places in the earth.
Earth, unexpected ally
Holding bones
That soldiers stuffed into you,
Holding – until the appointed time.

Hands grasping bone,
Naming the dead,
Blessing the dead,
Reburying the dead in a sacred manner.

Bones telling the truth,
Naming the atrocities,
Pointing at the soldiers -
Power in the bones – Life in the bones.

Wayne, Pennsylvania, August 1996

I've been back in the United States for one year. The distance from Nicaragua and its daily crisis has allowed me the space to grieve and mourn the many deaths and losses that I have carried in my body and soul.

I feel lighter now, as if part of my burden has been lifted. I have more energy for living. But there is still this stubborn sorrow that seems to reside just behind my eyes. It just hovers there like a mist and everything I see is filtered through it – tinged with a wash of sadness. It wraps itself around my smiles and times of happiness. It lingers in my soul. I try to block it out but it seeps through every barrier. I move away and it follows. I try to fill my mind with other thoughts but it jumbles and clouds them. I splash cold water in my face to wash it away but it persists. I have grieved my pain. Yet this somber, shadow sadness lingers in my soul and drifts through me like a ghost:

Carried on the breath of God,
I am the sadness of a generation that gave their lives –
lived everyday, thought every thought,
breathed every breath –
for a dream child – la niña roja y negra –
a revolutionary dream –
and then saw it destroyed.
I am the people's sadness
born out of witness to the passion –
the torture and death – of that dream.

She was born of all of you, nurtured and parented by you.
You loved her into life,
bringing your strengths and your weaknesses.
You loved her with passion – the way that I love you.
You delighted in her as I delight in you.
She was a MAGNIFICENT child.

Now give her to me –
the part that you still carry – every last bit of her.
I am passing through the souls of all who loved her,
gathering the threads they still carry.
Give the ones you are holding to me.
I will not be able to rest until
every thread of her is returned to me.
Then she will be rewoven into a new garment.
She will be made whole and given to you again.
Do not cling to her.

Spirit wants the fabric that I've got – this stinking wad of
blood encrusted fabric that I'm clinging to. She wants it back.
It belongs to her. But it's the only piece of that dream I have
left and I am not giving it up. Not yet.

Red Thread

Wayne, Pennsylvania, November 1996

Arnoldo Alemán has just been elected president of Nicaragua. He was a government official during the Somoza dictatorship. The wheel has turned full circle.

The martyrs lie silent in their graves. Their names, portraits and inspirational words have been whitewashed off the walls of Managua by a presidential decree. They seem to want to kill not only the body and the spirit but the memory as well. And they seem to be succeeding. There has been no resurrection of their bodies. The people are perishing once again. What is the point in loving, in dreaming, in struggling for the kingdom to come if it will only be destroyed? Was it all in vain?

I lie in a corner, licking my wounds like a bleeding dog that has been beaten by its master. The trauma of the master's cruelty is locked into every cell of my being so that I can no longer stand tall and proud. I can no longer run on strong legs or frolic, as I once did, delighting in my beauty and grace – delighting in my spirit. My spirit has been whipped into a corner where it huddles and trembles awaiting the next assault. All joy is gone. All beauty and strength have disappeared – only this grisly, trembling bundle of bones remains. And the pain of remembering how it used to be – the happiness, the joy, the exuberance, the delight in life. Why has God abandoned us to this hell master? Why does God allow us to be broken and beaten into submission?

The blood has dried hard and black on the gnarled fabric. It lies wadded up in the corner with me. It is ruined, ugly and cannot be repaired. I should throw it away, burn it. But I can't bring myself to let it go.

Spirit is back again. She's waiting for my piece of cloth. She's not leaving without it this time. I reach down deep into my soul and pull up the mass of bloodied threads that I carry there. It's all I have left of her. I hand them over to Spirit. A river of tears flows out behind them.

Oh, God! We tried so hard. We just couldn't keep her alive – a child can only take so much abuse. She died in our arms.

Spirit blows her breath on the child and once again she is alive in my arms. It is pure gift to hold her again; one last moment to remember all the possibility. But Spirit is calling her back and pulls her from me. The child shudders and sinks limply into my arms. She is motionless. There is no more breath. The warmth seeps out of her quickly. She is gone.

Spirit tells me to bury the body. I dig a hole for her in the earth with my hands. I lay her little, cold body down. Tears I've been stuffing down for years start to flow. These tears belong to her – to a revolution that I fell in love with. I cry the hole full of tears. Her little body lies again in a dark void full of salt water. May this burial womb be her passage into new life. With God's blessing, I seal her in with handfuls of earth. I pat a little round mound on top of her with the palms of my hands. I seal her with the Sign of the Cross.

I stand with my tears still streaming and I turn to my God, "I hate Your ways of living and dying. It hurts so badly. Take her. Damn it! Take her and make her live again!"

Wayne, Pennsylvania, January 1997

Our second daughter has been born. We name her Olivia, the bearer of peace. We've taken to calling her "Liv," for short. Our home echos with her mantra …Live …LIVe …LIVE!

Wayne, Pennsylvania, April 1997

A friend, Fr. Grant Gallup, is visiting from Managua. He brought word that Carmen has been kicked out of the cemetery in Paiwas. The new parish priest declared that all of the martyrs had to be removed from "consecrated ground." Carmen and half the population of the cemetery were exhumed and moved off church grounds.

In the same recounting, he also shared a rumor that he'd heard. It concerned Yamilett. It was said that she looked into Carmen's coffin when it was uncovered and was astounded because Carmen's face looked the same as the day they'd buried her. Impossible! In the rain forest, things rot in a day! That priest kicked a miracle out of his cemetery. He didn't realize it was SHE who consecrated the ground.

Wayne, Pennsylvania, July 1997

I continue to struggle with extreme contradictions. I received two letters today – one from a friend still working in Nicaragua and the other from my aunt in Washington D.C., with a newspaper clipping. My friend, Ellen, says that things have never been worse in Nicaragua. The country has resumed its status as the second poorest country in the hemisphere next to Haiti. Violence, gangs, drugs and prostitution are rampant. The streets are full of hungry children begging for food. The rain forest is in danger of being sold off to multinationals for lumber. Women languish in sweatshops, making blue jeans for K-Mart. Paramilitary squads have petitioned the National Assembly for legal status. Another drought has devastated the countryside. The Franciscan sisters have decided to leave their mission in the barrio because the times are so violent. Ellen says that she feels that every space possible in which to do something creative or life giving is being shut down. She says it feels like she is suffocating. She says I need to get very strong before I can come back.

The clipping from my aunt appeared on front page of *The Washington Post:*

OLLIE NORTH – ACTION HERO –
TEN YEARS AFTER IRAN-CONTRA,
FREEDOM ALLIANCE HONORS MR. RIGHT

It was exactly ten years ago this week that Lt. Col. Oliver North became an overnight sensation by testifying about his role in the arms-for-hostages scheme known as the Iran-Contra Affair. Call him a sentimental fool but last night North and his conservative friends threw an anniversary party "in celebration of Nicaraguan freedom and ultimate victory in the Cold War." There were thumbs up for Ronald Reagan, Democracy and God. It was a love fest for North. Celebrating Oliver North and his role in history reminds the world that Reagan was right about Nicaragua and Central America.

Wayne, Pennsylvania, September 1997

I continue to receive letter after letter about the worsening conditions in "free and democratic" Nicaragua. Friends seem overwhelmed and feel impotent in the face of such massive poverty and disempowerment. A recurring dream is haunting me. It comes at night and by day. Actually, it is ever-present except for the times I can keep busy enough to block it out.

In the dream, I see a small child sitting on a bare concrete floor. This is not the child of hopes and dreams that I buried. This is a living child. She is crying inconsolably. Her little face is streaked with tears and broken with pain. There is no one to comfort her. I ache and am afraid for this child. Where is her mother? Why is there no one to pick her up? I cannot bear her pain. I feel as if someone were pouring hot acid on my chest – searing my heart. I want to scream.

In my desperation, I go to her intending to gather her in my arms, to comfort her and to end her nightmare. But just as my hands are about to touch her, she is transformed into thousands of little children. THEY ARE ALL CRYING – all abandoned. They roam the streets of Managua, Calcutta, Port-au-Prince. They are begging, eating garbage, sleeping on concrete. They have gonorrhea and sniff glue out of Gerber baby food jars made in the United States of America.

I cannot hold them all. It is impossible. I am overwhelmed. They are too many to gather in my two arms. My arms fall back to my sides limply, aching in emptiness. The child remains sitting on the bare concrete floor – wailing – uncomforted.

I will not abandon this child. I will not walk away. Anyway, there is no escaping her – she's with me always. So I stand before her and let her shatter me in the crucible of her cry. My head falls back, my mouth opens wide and I cry with her. I wail with her. I am crying for help. I am begging for help.

Then the spirit of a man comes towards me. He is huge, dark – the color of the earth. He wears a single strand of white cowry shells around his neck. He is gentle and light. He sits on the bare concrete floor and gathers the child into his lap. He holds her. She melts into his embrace. The wailing softens and slows. She breathes deeply, sobs and draws another breath. There is silence. There is peace.

I stand in this peaceful silence and breathe it into the depths of my soul – deep, rich, fecund silence and peace that drips like honey from a jeweled goblet wrought of finest gold. It's a peace that can restore an entire garment by just pulling a single thread.

"Remember what the Mohawk woman told you?" he asks.

Yes. I remember. I had asked Chief Jake Swamp[25] and his wife, Judy, what sustained them in their work of peacemaking, disarmament and tree planting – given all that their people had endured. After a moment of silence, Judy had

---

[25] Jake Swamp is a spiritual leader, Sub-chief of the Wolf Clan for the Mohawk Nation. He and his wife, Judy, work with the Tree of Peace Society, an environmental organization established to continue a centuries-old Iroquois tradition of planting trees as symbols of peace.

said, *"The elders always taught us to keep the children in the center – never let them cry. That is the way. That is the answer."*

"Yes," the man says, *"pursue this in yourself and teach others. Keep this at the center and follow me."*

I know the spirit of this man. I know his way is hard. I am afraid of his way. I have two young daughters to care for and his way is not easy for a mother. I don't know where he will take me. I remember where he took Guillermo, Zunilda and Carmen.

He knows my thoughts and speaks to me again, "I will not abandon you. I will not leave you desolate. Follow me."

"But I don't know where you are going," I pleaded.

"Neither do I, my sister. I just know the way."

I trust and I take his hand...

...and following in "the way" – in faith – not being able to control exactly what that leads to ...my trust is restored.

Wayne, Pennsylvania, October 1997

I am not the same person I was when I first set foot on Nicaraguan soil in 1984. I have changed. At times I hardly recognize myself or what has happened to me. I have shed my veil of innocence – like a snake sheds its skin. The delicate white veil of my innocence is gone. I will never wear it again. What lies beneath is an older, weathered, toughened skin.

It is hard to get used to this new skin. I miss the veil and its naiveté, its tenderness, laughter and unspoiled optimism. I miss the way it sparkled and glistened on me like morning dew on a spider web. I miss the comfort of my all-powerful God who could part seas, strike people dead and fix everything if I only asked fervently enough. But that God changed also. The process of healing required that God to grow. I was led to other cultures, spiritual traditions, medicine ways and the beauty of nature in order to find the God that I needed.

Red Thread

Grandmother Spider, Bone Woman, the Woman who holds the cryin' ones, the Man the color of the earth – all of them reveal aspects of that which is Sacred, that which is Holy. A God much larger, more complex, more intimate and a greater mystery than I had ever imagined has been revealed to me.

So I stand in this new skin and take a long look at myself – trying to understand the changes. In this skin I feel slower, more deliberate, wiser, deeper. It hangs heavier, like a cloak. I can pull the sides of it around me when my eyes are sore from too much pain. I can heal in the dark silent folds of its rich fabric. I have reclaimed a sacred space and learned to protect it by setting clear spiritual, emotional and physical boundaries. I protect it by being very intentional about the context and risks attendant to actions I might take. I safe-guard it by clearing pain and negativity so as not to hold them inside and additionally, by balancing exposure to violence with immersion in that which restores life and creativity. Fi-nally, I care for my sacred space by listening to my intuition, body and dreams for guidance. In this skin, I have learned how to work for the healing of suffering and violence in the world without being overwhelmed by it.

In this skin I know that the process of healing is an ardu-ous yet beautiful one that has restored and deepened my trust in a loving God. I have learned that my connection to Creator must be kept strong and alive – like an umbilical cord – thick, pulsating with lifeblood. In this skin I know how to nourish and protect this cord that connects me to that which gives and sustains life – to that in which we move and have our being. She is my power. She is the source of red thread that I have been trying to reach...color of blood...color of life. I am spinning out Red Thread.

"Myselves the grievers grieve...and miracles cannot atone," etching by Judith Anderson, photo by Jim Colando

This journal is about remembering, mourning, healing, reconstructing, re-empowerment and ultimately resurrection.

AFTERWORD

This journal is about remembering, mourning, healing, re-constructing, re-empowerment and ultimately resurrection. Even in the absence of repentance on the part of the perpetrators of violence, the journey from victimization to resurrection still happens. It happens in each and every one of us who spins out our knotted, bloodied thread until it comes out thick, healed and full of life again. It happens when we re-connect with that which is sacred and with the sources of creativity in our lives. It happens when we take the hand of that which creates and sustains life and keep walking.

This resiliency is visible in many individual lives, communities and social processes in Nicaragua: in the women's movement working for a society free of violence in all of its forms; in the tenacity of those who educate about and defend human rights; in healers and centers for natural medicine all over the country; in the *campesinos* practicing biological agriculture and reforestation; in conversations about sustainable development; in the first university to be established on the Atlantic Coast; in sister cities that continue to build bridges between people; and in reconciliation work. There are spinners of red thread in efforts to protect Nicaragua's endangered natural resources and the rights of Indigenous peoples. There are spinners of red thread accompanying the street children and in the children of *Acahualinca*, the garbage dump of Managua, who dance like the wind and perform at The National Theater.

Spinners of red thread are remembering, mending what has been torn, witnessing so that it doesn't happen again, holding the cryin' ones, placing the children in the center and weaving anew the fabric of life.

OTHER BOOKS FROM EPICA

Oscar Romero: Memories in Mosaic, by María López Vigil (EPICA, 2000) 424 pages, $19.95

The Story of a Great Love: Life with the Guatemalan "Communities of Population in Resistance," A Spiritual Journal by Ricardo Falla, SJ. (EPICA, 1998) 132 pages, $12.95

The Economic Way of the Cross/Vía Crucis Económico (EPICA, Witness for Peace, and the Religious Working Group on the World Bank and the IMF, 1999, 2000) Bilingual, 112 pages, $6.50

Guatemala: The Certainty of Spring, by Julia Esquivel (EPICA, 1993) Bilingual, 188 pages, $11.95

Voices and images: Mayan Ixil Women of Chajul by The Association of Mayan Ixil Women (ADMI, 2000) Trilingual, 111 pages, $35.00

Ask about our Women's Series as well!
Write, call or email us today for a free catalog:

EPICA
Ecumenical Program on Central America & the Caribbean
1470 Irving Street, NW
Washington, DC 20010
epicabooks@igc.org
202/332-0292